THE M WORD

By

Eileen Wharton

First published in 2018 by Bombshell Books

www.bombshellbooks.com

Print ISBN 978-1-912604-47-0

Also By Eileen Wharton

Shit Happens
Blanket of Blood

Praise For Eileen Wharton

"Razor sharp wit and comical descriptions are used to good effect by the author to create a novel that guarantees a chortle a chapter." **Darren Sant - Goodreads**

"A first class read and highly recommended." Kay Robinson **- Goodreads**

"A brilliant read and another one of those books you just cannot put down." - **Amazon Reviewer**

"I found this a real page turner. Exciting, scary, touching, funny. All emotions in spades." **Amazon Reviewer**

"Would make a wonderful telly series. Funny, naughty, with an entertaining heroine." **Amazon Reviewer**

"Hats off to Ms Wharton for a great entrance into the crime genre!" **Noelle Holten - Crimebookjunkie**

"A very well written and enjoyable book- highly recommended." **Misfits Farm - Goodreads**

"There are enough red herrings to lead the reader astray, and my imagination was working overtime as I tried to piece this well plotted puzzle together..." **Lorraine Rugman - The Book Review Cafe**

"The overall plot is fantastic - deliciously dark and creepy - I loved it and can't wait for the sequel." **KA Richardson - Author**

"Lovers of serial killer thrillers will enjoy this book. Well written with great characterisation." **Lisa - Goodreads**

Chapter 1

@RobertaGallbreath
#Restingbitchface
#Flissflop

'Mother is dying,' a voice on the house phone says.

'Who is this?' I ask.

'It's Fliss, who do you think it is?'

'Let me see. It's three years since I spoke to you last, Felicity, so I wasn't expecting to pick up the phone and hear *your* voice.'

'Are you coming or not?' my sister snaps.

'Where?'

'Home, of course. She's dying, Roberta. Even you must care about that.' What's with the *even you* shit? Why do people say that? My sister is good at emotional blackmail. 'She's asking for you. God knows why.'

'How long?'

'Days rather than weeks. Doctor said to gather the family. Can you tell Carolyn and Shoni?'

'And Drew,' I say. Silence. 'He didn't do it, Felicity.'

'Whatever.'

'I know my own son.' Silence. 'He might be a lot of things, but he's not a thief.'

'I didn't ring to argue with you. Just get here, will you.'

'I'll come tomorrow,' I say. She hangs up.

My sister's a bitch. Don't get me wrong, I'm not all sweetness and light myself, but Felicity is a witch and a martyr, and there's nothing more unattractive than the smell of burning martyr. She stayed with Mother when she could have left to live in Bermuda with a police officer from Pocklington she had met on eHarmony. She's bitter and twisted, and let's face it, who wouldn't be, living with Mother all those years?

#nilbymouth

Mother's on form. Even on her deathbed, she can make me feel like crap. She sits up in bed, her grey curls flattened by the pillows she's now propped on, winceyette bed jacket draped around her spiky shoulders, "ALICE GALLBREATH: NIL BY MOUTH" at her head.

'Don't know why *you* bothered coming all the way up here,' she says.

'It's only twenty minutes up the road.'

'Why do I never see you, then? There's nowt for you in t' will.'

'I don't want anything, Mother,' I say.

'That'll be a first. Stand up straight and put your legs together. You couldn't stop a pig in a passage.'

'Stop with the compliments, will you?' I say.

'What you doing here?'

'I came to see you.'

'Want to watch me die?'

'No, Mother. I came to say my goodbyes.'

'Goodbye, then.'

'Jesus, can you not just…'

'What? Just what?' Mother asks.

'Just be nice,' I say.

'That's rich, coming from you.'

'Look, I know I haven't been the World's Best Daughter,' I say.

'Pah. Understatement of the year. Get one of those thingies from the nurse, will you?'

'Thingies? Which nurse?'

'The one that's plain as a pikestaff. I need to say a decade of the rosary every time I look at her… A thingummy jig whatsit doodah…' She sets off coughing, and I think she's going to choke to death there and then. She waves her hand madly in the direction of the cupboard next to the bed.

'In here?' I ask. She nods. 'A tissue?' She nods again. I hand her a tissue, and she spits into it. Fresh red blood mixed with black swirls like a marble. She folds the tissue, shoves it into my hand and gestures to the plastic bag taped to her locker. I try not to retch as I stuff it in. 'You haven't exactly been Mum of the Year, either.'

'Go on, kick me while I'm down.'

'I'm not here to kick you, Mother. Felicity said you were asking for me.'

'Yes, I wanted you to know that I know who took the money and your father's watch, and I want you to get it back.'

'Listen, if you're going to accuse Drew again, I–'

'I'm not.'

'That was a terrible time for us…'

'I wasn't going to accuse Drew,' she says. 'I know it wasn't Drew. He wouldn't nick off his granny. I want you to get it back. I still want Drew to have it.'

'Who was it?'

'I don't want it to cause trouble. I just want you to get it back.'

'From where, Mother? Where do I get it from?'

'Fliss,' she says faintly.

'I don't understand. What about Felicity?'

'It wasn't your dad's watch. Well, it was. But not the man you thought was your dad.'

'What do you mean? What are you talking about? You're talking in riddles. Whose was it? Mother?'

'The letters explain,' she says, her breath shallow and laboured.

'Letters? What letters?'

'In there,' she says, pointing to the bedside cabinet. 'They explain.'

'Explain what?'

'Everything. They explain everything. Forgive me…'

Her breath grows ragged, and the machine beside her beeps. A nurse comes running. It's all a bit of a blur after that. Doctors run in. They shock her, and her heart starts again, then stops. They shock her again, calling, 'Alice, Alice, can you hear me, Alice?'

When I've seen paramedics performing CPR on the telly, it's so clean and clinical. This is brutal. Messy, noisy, the sound of ribs cracking, a blue mouth foaming, eyes rolling.

It seems like hours before a man in a white coat shakes his head and says, 'Time of death, eleven twenty-two am.'

I can't say that what I feel is sadness, but there is shock. Definite shock. Seeing Mother silent and not deadly. I wouldn't say she looks peaceful or that she looks like she's sleeping. She looks dead. Bitter Alice. Deceased. What did she want to explain? What did she want me to forgive?

I open her bedside cabinet and take out a brown bag. Inside is a bundle wrapped in red cloth. Unwinding the material, I can see letters, a huge bundle of letters, held together by elastic bands. I stuff them into my bag, intending to read them when I get home.

I sit beside the bed in a state of shock until Felicity arrives and blames me for killing our mother. 'I think, in fact, that it was lung cancer that killed her.'

'She was alright last night,' she says. 'She was chatting about Freda Birchill's granddaughter being done for shoplifting.'

'She wasn't alright, though, was she? You called me up here because she was dying. You said to me that she didn't have long left.'

'Yeah, but I didn't think…that she would really die.' Her face crumples then, and I feel almost sorry for her. I put my hand on her shoulder, and she shrugs it off. 'Do you think it's been fun looking after her for the past twenty years while you swanned off to the city? You, the big I am.'

'It's Newcastle, Felicity, not New York. If you wanted a life, you could have chosen one.'

'Chosen? Chosen?' Her voice rises, and she beats her chest. 'I didn't have choices. My path was paved when you left. I couldn't leave as well, could I? She'd have been on her own.'

I ignored her self-pity party. 'She mentioned the money and Granddad's watch. She said she knew Drew didn't take it.'

'If you've come here to cause trouble, I swear I'll …'

'Do what? Fliss, you invited me to come.'

'Just go back to where you came from.'

'I came from here, actually.'

'So why do you talk as though you have a mouth full of marbles?'

'What is it you want from me, Felicity?'

'Nothing. I want nothing. Precisely what you've given me over the years.'

'I'm going back,' I say. 'Let me know the arrangements for the funeral.'

'Oh, yes, leave it all to me as usual. You can tell Drew to stay away, for a start.'

'I'll tell him no such thing. And I'll tell you another thing, Mother wants him to have his granddad's watch. Well, she said it's not Dad's. So, what do you know about that?'

'Nothing. I've no idea what you're talking about.'

'She wants me to find the watch and give it to Drew, and that's what I'm going to do.' Her face turns red, then green, then white. She storms off, sticking her nose in the air.

Chapter 2

#Karmachameleon

I know you'll think I'm cold and hard. I haven't shed a tear over Mother. I'm not sure what I feel. If, indeed, I feel anything at all. Maybe I'm in shock. Maybe I'm numb, and when the numbness wears off, I'll be a blubbering mess of tears and snot. I'm generally not an emotional person, though. I'm stoic. Impassive. Heartless, some say. I'm certainly not the most patient of people, I don't suffer fools gladly, and I'm not politically correct. I'm not a do-gooder or a tree hugger, and I pretty much hate everyone. At least I'm consistent.

I have decided, however, that today, I am going to change. I am going to try to be good and kind. To myself and others. I intend to save up some Karma before that bitch comes around to slap me in the face. Death can do that to a person. It makes you take stock. It makes you want to be better.

I left for work with the intention of being positive. Then, my menopausal car wouldn't start. She overheated as soon as the engine turned over. I knew how she felt, but it was very frustrating to have to take the bus and mingle with the plebs. Why couldn't everything just run smoothly?

I was called into the office. The boss, Oldham (appropriate name cos he smells of rancid meat), said I have to make more of an effort to be congenial. That's rich coming from him, the most curmudgeonly old codger I've ever come across. Before you ask, I don't fancy him. He's old enough to be my dad, and his face looks like a corned beef sandwich left out in the rain. He said my mood swings were becoming intolerable, and I'd better pull my socks up or else. I haven't worn socks since I was thirteen and I used them to pad my bra. *My* mood swings? Or else *what*?

It transpired, after listening to the middle-aged morons in the canteen, the mood swings may be a symptom of something else. I thought perhaps it was PMS: Pre-Menstrual Syndrome. Symptoms ranged from having a heightened sense of smell to wanting to kill my firstborn for breathing. When my periods stopped, I should have realised. Not that I miss bleeding for eight days a month. But, really? The M word? At my age?

It's all downhill from here. And I didn't even notice the zenith.

#saggymammaries

Last night, I ate a Domino's pizza, four Curly Wurlies and a family size bag of Doritos. I wake up feeling bloated and deflated. Talk about oxymoron. I realise I have nothing to look forward to but saggy boobs, dry patches and a moustache. Death makes you think about your own mortality. Seeing Mother looking so old and frail made me realise that one day, I'd be like that.

I take a selfie, then regret it. I look like a bloated cow. Even Photoshop doesn't improve it, so I Snapchat it to Tammy with the caption, "Kill me now". She sends back a picture of her and her trout pout looking like a beauty queen with the caption, "ALOTBSOL BAE". I haven't a clue what she's talking about most of the time.

Work is a challenge. Mick the Dick is being his usual smug self. He catches me at the water cooler and asks me what I'm doing at the weekend. I lie and say I have plans with friends.

'You going to the company ball?' he asks.

'Dunno,' I say.

The company ball happens once a year. They hire a castle and a marquee. Everyone gets paralytic on the free booze and ends up canoodling among the conifers. I've had enough drunken office fumbles to last a lifetime.

'You're not one of these boring people who don't go, are you?'

'I'm not boring at all,' I say.

'Good, I'll look forward to seeing you there then. You taking a date?'

'Em…er…yeah,' I lie. Shit. Shit. Why did I have to do that? Now, I can't turn up without a man in tow. He looks me up and down.

'Oh well,' he says.

'What's that supposed to mean?' I say. The bloody cheek of it.

***

'I've got to show him,' I tell Tammy later. 'I have to have the hottest date there!'

'How the hell are you going to manage that?'

'You're going to help me,' I say.

I eye myself in the full-length mirror. I used to think middle-age spread was something you put on toast. I now realise it's the devil at work, turning pert breasts and bottoms into coconut haystacks and things that look like they've been hit with a shovel. Luckily, I'm not one of those square-bottomed girls. Not yet, at least. Mine's still round. Very round. Like a barrage balloon in a full moon.

Everything used to be so pert and well formed. Now, if I walk round with my bra off, I get a rub rash on my knees. Lift the hem of your jeans to show your nips type thing. The trouble is, inside, I'm still that sexy siren who's size six and a *femme fatale*. It's only when I pass a mirror or see a photo that the disillusionment descends.

There was a time when I was so gorgeous, I didn't just turn heads, I turned gay men. Now, it seems I'm turning milk sour and straight men away.

I used to be irritated by men whistling at me from building sites. Now, it gives me a thrill, a frisson of excitement, until I realise they're ogling the pretty young thing walking behind me. Sexist bastards!

I'm depressed about weight gain, so I eat a tub of Phish Food and four Cadbury's Creme Eggs washed down with a litre of Rioja. Grapes are good for you, right?

I suddenly remember Mother's letters. I unwrap the dusty bundle from the red cloth and release the envelopes from their elastic prison. They smell musty, like old lofts and abandoned railway carriages.

Letter number one:

10th November, 1940

Dear Michael,

The days are long here on my own. I wish I could have stayed in London with you and Mother and Father. I wouldn't have minded the blacked-out windows, the sirens and the bombs dropping. I'd have relished leaving the air-raid shelter with the acrid smell of smoke in the air and the buildings crumpled around us, if it meant I could be with you. Being separated makes me feel like only half a person.

We'd have played hide-and-seek in the rubble; we'd have cheeked the warden and run rings round his stout belly as he tried in vain to catch us; we'd have fooled the butcher into giving us extra pigs' feet; we'd have dreamt of bananas, yellow and exotic as half a sun.

Part of me feels angry at Mother and Father for separating us. And part feels angry at you for contracting TB. Though

I know in my rational moments that it's not your fault and that you didn't want to be separated, either. I know you were too ill to make the train journey and though the air here is probably better for your chest (but judging by smell alone, you wouldn't think so. The whole place smells of shit. Cow dung, horse manure, dog dirt), I understand why Mother wished you to stay there. I just wish she'd let me stay, too, until you were well enough for us to travel together.

Perhaps the Mister and Missus might be kinder if you were here. There's safety in numbers. Perhaps you could talk their daughters into being civil to me. One look at your smile and they'd be soft as cow muck in your hands. As it is, they are beasts. They pull my hair and spit in my food.

At least the food's better here. We get fresh eggs from the chickens and rabbit stew. The rabbits are caught by the local boys and swapped for eggs and milk. There's a never-ending supply of fresh vegetables from the allotments. We don't get fruit unless it's nicked from old Mrs Flanagan's orchard. Those apples taste sweeter than any I've ever known. Not as sweet as the sight of your face will be when you get off the train at Durham station. I will come and meet you, if the Missus will let me away from my chores. My list is endless. Cinderella has nothing on me.

The other kids make fun of the way I speak. They say I'm posh and la-di-dah. Bloody hell's fire! Posh and la-di-dah is something we'd never be called at home.

Counting the days until you get here,

Love,

Alice

Dear Alice,

I don't know whether you'll get this, but Mother says I can write to you, and she'll post it. Sorry you're having a hard time down there. It ain't the best here, yet strangely, we're all pulling together and the atmosphere's electric. I'm feeling much better, and hopefully, I'll soon be coming to meet you.

There was an air raid last night, and we were all shunted into the underground station. We were packed in like sardines. We were next to the Irish family from our street. Mr McKinnon played tunes on his accordion, and we all sang along. We could hear the bombs echo down the lift shaft which was the washing facilities and toilets. We were worried they would burst a water main and we'd get flooded, but the singing took our minds off it.

When we were allowed back above ground, whole streets had disappeared and, in their place, lay smoking piles of rubble. We heard that Charlie White's whole family had been wiped out, and only Charlie was left. We all clubbed together and bought him a Meccano set. I'll never forget the forlorn look on his face as he clutched the gift while he was bundled into a coach and sent off to live with relatives he's never met. Cor blimey, the kid looked like he'd lost a pound and found a penny. Wish you were here.

Your loving brother,
Michael

I can't believe Mother had a brother and told us nothing about him. She always maintained she was an only child. To say I'm stunned is an understatement.

Letter number two:
14th September, 1940
Dear Michael,
I wish you'd hurry up. The kids round here are all dunces and scatterbrains. Every time I speak, they mimic me. It's pathetic. The boys would run a mile if you were here to take my side. I'm sure you could melt the icy hearts of the Mister and Missus. My God, they are miserable folk. You'd think that living in the countryside would make people cheerful. I always imagined

them all whistling along to the birds and milking cows with a cheery song bursting from their fresh-air-filled lungs. He mainly grunts, and she shrieks with the pitch of broken chalk on a blackboard. Never does a smile sit on their lips, never a laugh escapes from their bellies.

I go to sleep imagining what fun we'll have. What larks.

Yours,
Alice

Tucked between the next two letters are yellowing pages torn from an exercise book. I recognise the handwriting immediately. It's mine. Where and when did Mother get hold of my diary? I can't believe she kept it all these years.

22nd September, 1979

Dear Diary,

I wish I had never been born. School today was hell on legs. Amanda Grimshaw and her cronies took the piss out of my shoes. 'Look at Gallbreath in her fake Pods and knee-high socks. Can you not afford a proper pair? Knee-high socks are for babies.' When I asked Mother for a proper pair of Pods and ankle socks, she slapped my face and called me an ungrateful wretch. She said, 'Other kids would be glad of those shoes. Kids in Africa have to walk miles to school in bare feet.' They'd have been welcome to my fake Pods. I didn't say this, as I imagined Mother would strike me again. She's got a hard hand. I still have the red handprint on the back of my thighs where she struck me last week for throwing my Brussels sprouts over next door's wall. It seems their dog is allergic, and the Hamptons have been faced with a huge vet's bill that Mother must contribute towards. How was I to know the stupid mutt wasn't vegetarian? Mrs Sheldon's dog will eat anything.

Felicity doesn't understand. She doesn't have it as hard as I do. Mother's friend, Theresa, has a girl a bit bigger than

Felicity, and she gets all her old clothes. She goes to a different school, too, so no one knows Fliss wears hand-me-downs. The mean girls and the popular girls like her because she fits in.

The teasing about my clothes was one thing but humiliating me in front of Alistair Cockburn, when they knew I had a crush on him, was just cruel. Mother's coming, so I need to put the light out.
More later,
R

14th February, 1980
Dear Diary,
It pains me to tell you about the Alistair Cockburn thing, but who else can I tell? I sent him a Valentine card. I've never sent one before, but I really like him. I daydream about holding his hand and sitting beside him on the bench at lunchtime. The bench is where all the people with boyfriends sit. Kind of showing off to the rest of the school that they're not sad and single. Except the ones who've been going out for yonks, and they go behind the gym. Not sure what they do there, but it's definitely stuff that they can't do on the bench. Gary Wilson stands guard, and if any of us get too close, he calls us perverts and threatens to beat us up. I don't want to go behind the gym. I'm a bit worried about what happens. I wouldn't have a clue what to do. Where do you learn this stuff? Are there classes somewhere? If there are, no one's ever invited me. I feel like everyone in the whole school knows something I don't.

Anyway, back to Alistair and the Valentine card. I don't know how to act in these situations. There are so many unwritten rules. The only time you put your name on a card is if you're already going out with the person. How was I supposed to know this? So, I sent the card and signed it, "love from Roberta." There was a handwritten verse inside. I love you, I love you, I love you almighty. I wish your pyjamas were next to my nightie. Don't be mistaken, don't be misled. I mean on the clothesline, not on the bed. How was I to know he'd show the card to his friends who would pass it round all the mean girls? I couldn't have known that they'd spend the rest of the day taunting me about it and singing the verse.

I hate them all.

I can't tell a teacher. I can't tell Mother. I just have to suffer.
More later,
R

28th February, 1980
Dear Diary,
Stupid mean girls are still singing the song from the Valentine card. Why won't they just leave me alone? I'm sitting in front of Mother on the hard floor having my hair raked with the nit comb when she asks me what's wrong.

'Nothing's wrong,' I say.

'Tell your face that,' she says.

'Just having a bit of trouble with some girls at school,' I say. I'm hoping for a hug, some kind words, maybe. I don't know why I'm wishing that. It's never happened before. Perhaps she'll march up to the school like Sharon Kell's mother, bowl into assembly and swear at the teachers until they cane "the little bastards who are picking on" her daughter.

'You'd better stick up for yourself,' she says, tugging my hair as hard as she can. 'Don't let them pick on you. Do you hear? If I hear that you've let them pick on you, I'll leather you, do you understand me?'

'Yes, Mother.' Thanks for the compassion.

The next time they launch a campaign of ridicule and hatred towards me, I vow to do as Mother says and stand up for myself.
More later,
R

I remember thinking I was very sophisticated keeping a diary. I first got the idea from a Judy Blume novel where the heroine, Margaret, talks to God about her problems. I thought I'd kept the blue exercise books well hidden. I wonder when Mother had found it, and why she'd kept it?

Dear Diary,
I learned a new word today: Menstruation. Menstrual cycle. It's nothing to do with men, however. Why didn't my mother tell me about periods? It would have been easy. She could have explained that women lay eggs (a bit like chickens, but we don't make omelettes from them). She could have said, as Julie Dinsdale's mother said, that each month girls have something called "the curse". Where you bleed for five to seven days, but don't die. She could have told me that Mother Nature sends a plague. Anything to warn me. Instead, I'm left screaming from the toilet cubicle that I'm going to die, and when I'm found there by Amanda Grimshaw and Theresa Duff, I'm shaking like an epileptic having a fit. They kick the door which swings wide open to show my bloody knickers round my ankles and my head in my hands.

'What the hell's wrong with you?' Theresa asks.

'I'm bleeding.'

'You got your period,' she says.

'My, what?' I say.

'She doesn't even know what her period is,' says Theresa spitefully. 'You really are a retard, Gallbreath.'

'How can you not know?' Amanda says, looking at me like she's just stood in something nasty.

It wouldn't be so bad, but they tell the whole class by the end of break time and the whole school by the end of the day.

'We're gonna call you Carrie from now on,' Amanda says.

'My name's not Carrie,' I say, remembering Mother's warning to stand up for myself.

'You really are a retard,' Theresa says.

I hate the stupid, spiteful little cows, Diary. I wish they'd never been born. If I knew where to get a weapon or how to use one, I'd kill them. I'm now reading a chapter in the Judy Blume novel which tells me about puberty and periods. If only I'd read it yesterday!

I'm sitting in my bedroom listening to the Bee Gees, and my eyes have sprung a leak. I feel so alone. Fliss is at a party that everyone but me is invited to. Mother asked me why I wasn't going, and instead of telling her I wasn't invited (because I had nettles in the back of my throat, and my eyes had pins and needles, and if I spoke about how unpopular I am, I might burst into tears, and Mother will slap me and tell me to stop causing a drama), I said I had lots of homework to do. She shouted at me that I shouldn't let the homework build up, and if there were any bad reports on parents' night, so help her God, she would leather me.

The Bee Gees are making me cry even more. My life's a bloody tragedy. I'm all alone, and I've got no soul.

Chapter 3

Reading passages from my diary takes me back all those years, and when the doorbell calls me back to the present, I notice my cheeks are wet, and I'm sobbing for my teenage self. I wonder if any of those toxic girls lie awake at night and feel guilty about the crap they put me through. I heard Theresa Duff was up the duff before we even got our O-Level results. I imagine her living on a council estate with a man named Sid who drives a Corsa and signs on the dole. She has six kids and spends her days watching *Judge Rinder* and reruns of *Sixteen and Pregnant.*

I wonder whether Mother felt guilty reading what I'd gone through. Why had she never mentioned it? If I'd read something like that from Carolyn or Shoni's diary, I'd have felt terrible. Wouldn't I? I need to make more effort with my kids. I need to be more maternal. I realise, even though I pretend to be a strong, confident, independent woman, all I've ever wanted is a man to love me. What's that about? I will never admit that to anyone. It's pathetic. I'm pathetic.

I shove the letters into a bag, wipe my eyes and open the door. Tammy shoves past me. 'How are you?' she asks.

'I'm an orphan,' I say as she plucks a bottle of Prosecco from her bag. 'A single, sad-sack orphan who's going to be alone forever.'

'Oh dear, we are feeling sorry for ourselves. I'll pour us a drink.'

'I have to find a decent date for the company ball or Mick will be smug for the rest of his sad little life. I can't bear it.'

She pops open the bubbly, pours us each a glass and passes me mine, clinking her glass against it and muttering, 'Cheers.' I can see her mind ticking over as she slurps the yellow liquid. She's one of those friends who is always setting you up with her friend's brother or her brother's friend. She was the one who made me join Match.com.

'You're never going to get fixed up, because you never go anywhere. And before you say anything, the laundrette and McDonalds don't count.'

'I bet some people have met their other half in Maccy D's. Love among the limp lettuce, bonking over burgers, frisky with fries.'

'You need a high-born man of quality. Someone with class.'

'I used to go out with a maths teacher,' I say.

'Not that kind of class,' she says. 'Who wants to talk about the square on the hypotenuse when you're about to climax?' She needn't have worried. I haven't climaxed once. 'I've got it,' she says.

'Chlamydia?' I ask.

'The answer to your love life.'

I throw her a disbelieving look.

'We need to get on Tinder.'

'What's Tinder?'

'You are so Victorian,' she says. 'It's a dating app.'

'Oh no,' I say. 'I'm still recovering from the last round of internet dating.'

'This is different.'

'You said that about PlentyOfFish, and I nearly drowned.'

'You're so dramatic. We have to get back out there, or we'll never find our soulmate.'

'Humpft. I don't want a soulmate.' A lie. I do. I just don't want to put myself out there and risk getting hurt. Again.

'I'm serious, Roberta. My biological clock is ticking.'

'Er, I think it's safe to say that clock has already stopped.'

'It's alright for you. You've had the pleasure of having three children.'

'What bloody pleasure?'

'Come on, you must have enjoyed some parts of it.'

'It was ok when they were at school.'

'You don't mean that, Roberta. I bet you loved them when they were little and newborn, dressed in white babygros and smelling of innocence.'

'I only remember them smelling of sick and crying all night.'

That wasn't altogether true. There had been difficult times when they were babies.

My ex-husband, Andy (who shall henceforth be known as Knobhead) used to disappear and leave me alone with them for days on end while he went fishing or camping or golfing. He liked things ending in -ing. Screwing Terri-Ann from Thomas Cook being one of them. But there had also been happy times, proud moments, fun times until Knobhead ruined it all.

All I seem to remember are the bad times. Crying myself to sleep while he and the bitch took my kids away for the weekend and bought them presents. That feeling of utter dejection and emptiness when he drove off, and the kids didn't even wave out of the back window of the car. And when they came home, they'd be full of how wonderful Terri-Ann was. I imploded with jealousy.

'Come on, Roberta,' Tammy says, bringing me back to the present. 'Even if we meet someone to bang.'

'I had more bang from last year's Christmas crackers than I've had with internet dating. And I bought them from Poundland. They were floppy and soggy. Story of my sex life.'

'I'm telling you,' she says, putting down her drink and picking my phone up from the coffee table, flicking through the apps. 'Tinder is what we need.' She spends the next ten minutes swearing at the screen while she downloads the app and then sets up a profile using my Facebook page.

'You might want to rethink your profile pic,' she says. 'Let's do a sexy one. Pull your top down.' She tugs at my cami to reveal more cleavage. 'And do a sexy pout. No, the pout's not going to work. You have a resting bitch face.'

'Cheers.'

'Smile instead,' she says, pointing my own phone in my face. 'People like to see a smiley face. It makes you look more approachable. Hmm, no, you look like you've got wind.' She clicks a few times then flicks through the pics. 'I could work with that one,' she says. 'I'll download an app to touch it up a bit. Make you look a bit more human. A bad profile pic means an immediate left swipe.'

'Left swipe? Dare I ask?'

'People swipe to the left if they're not interested and to the right if they are. A left swipe is the equivalent of being left on the bench at the school disco. I imagine you know what that feels like?'

'Remind me again, why are we friends?' I ask.

'Because no one else likes you,' she says.

'Again, cheers.'

'Only I know that your bark is worse than your bite.'

'I haven't bitten you yet,' I say.

'You're a real softie deep down. Very deep,' she says. 'If you would just let people in once in a while.'

'Let people in? Why? So they can break my heart?'

'I knew it,' Tammy says. 'I knew that was the reason you come across as so hard. It's because you're really soft. Deep down you're scared, Roberta Gallbreath. You're just like the bloody rest of us. You're terrified of being hurt.'

'Bollocks,' I say.

She's right, of course. Deep down, I am bloody scared. Having your heart broken is more painful than breaking any bones. Six weeks in plaster and a course of physio can't fix it. For two full years, I screamed inside while Knobhead lived in blissful happiness with that tart of a travel agent. Two years wondering what I'd done wrong. I'd cooked and cleaned, brought up his children single-handedly, massaged his feet and his ego, all to be dropped like a shitty stick because he couldn't keep it in his trousers.

'You'll have your day,' my friends had said. 'He'll come crawling back, and you'll be able to kick him in the teeth.' But he didn't come crawling back, and I never saw my day. He just looked happier and happier, and I got more and more miserable, hating everybody and everything. 'Karma will get him in the end,' they'd said. Those happy, settled friends whose mortgages were paid and whose kids were heading for medical school. There I was, trying to keep body and soul together by living on potato skins and offal, while he and the tart of a travel agent were travelling to London business class and eating at The Ivy.

My heart completely shattered when I met her in town and she was buying nappies, her swollen stomach giving away the secret my kids had been warned to keep from me. That hurt more than anything else. I couldn't even slap her then for all the pain she'd put me through. Who wanted to be the person arrested for assaulting a pregnant woman?

That was when I finally knew he wasn't coming back. I took to my bed for three weeks until a teenage Carolyn came, opened the blinds, threw out the congealed plates and made me take a shower. 'You've wallowed long enough, Mother,' she said. 'Time to get your life back.'

I started with walks to the park. The sunlight was blinding after having spent so long down the well of my misery. I jumped at the sound of traffic and blushed when people spoke to me. Going back to work was hell on legs. People avoided the water cooler when I was standing there; they took long cigarette breaks, and silence descended when I entered a room. I was the loony old female cuckold, best avoided. I became surly and disinterested. If people didn't want to be around me, I wouldn't be around them. I threw myself into my work and became very successful at what I did. Work became a substitute for love.

'Ok, this pic is sooo important,' Tammy says. 'It's the first thing men will see of you. You have to look approachable, attractive and sexy, or they won't even look at your profile. It's much more ruthless than Match.com or PlentyOfFish.' She taps away on my screen. 'There are unspoken rules. Not too many selfies, use some holiday snaps, a couple with sunglasses are ok, but we want to see your eyes, maybe one with a puppy…'

'I'm allergic to dogs,' I say. 'Take one of me with a puppy and I'll look like the Fly.'

'A couple of group shots. Not too many,' Tammy twitters away to herself. 'You don't want him to have to play Where's Wally, but it'll show you have friends.' *Tap, tap, tap*. 'Right, the bio needs to be short. What shall I say about you?' *Tap, tap, tap*. 'That should do it. I think we're ready to roll.' She passes me my phone, complete with Tinder app and my new profile.

'That picture is awful,' I say, pointing to a holiday snap of me in a low-cut cami, sitting by the pool drinking sangria.

'Best of a bad bunch,' she says. 'I have to work with what I had. "Can't make a silk purse out of a sow's arse," my grandad used to say. I wanted them to see that you like to travel. It shows you're not narrow-minded. Ok, let's get swiping. Remember, swipe right if you like and left to lose.' It would help if I knew my right from my left.

I look at the men's pictures popping up in front of me. 'Tammy, I have leftover pizza older than these guys. What the hell are you trying to do to me?'

'Give it here,' she says, snatching the phone. 'I'll reset your age range. Jeez, you've got no sense of adventure.'

'You've got no sense of decorum or decency.'

'Rubbish. Age is just a number.' A man posing with a lion pops up. I swipe left. Another with his obviously ex-girlfriend cut from the picture – left again. One with sixteen selfies, all with him wearing flowered shirts and sunglasses – left. Another left. Tammy snatches the phone from my hand and says, 'There's nothing wrong with him.' She swipes right. I reach for the phone, and she holds it at arm's length, swiping right again.

'Give it back,' I say.

'Ooh, you've got a match,' she says. 'He looks quite dishy.'

I peek. 'Yeah, if you like a dog's dinner.'

'Don't be cruel. Ooh, you've got a message.' A message comes up on the screen.

'ARE YOUR FEET SORE?' I look at Tammy, and she shrugs her shoulders.

I type, 'No, why?'

'BECAUSE YOU'VE BEEN RUNNING THROUGH MY MIND ALL NIGHT.'

'Tammy, what the f…'

'You just have to weed out the losers,' she says. 'It just takes a bit of effort, that's all. Keep swiping.'

'I'll bloody swipe you,' I say. 'This is the worst idea you've ever had. Even worse than the gold lamé tracksuit that made you look like Jimmy Savile's younger sister.'

'I loved that shell suit,' she says. 'It was cutting edge. Everyone loved it at the time.'

'Hmm, they all loved Jimmy Savile, too, and look what happened there.'

I continued to swipe left for loser.

'The more you swipe right, the more chance you have of meeting someone appropriate. In the meantime, you could practise your chat,' Tammy says.

'I've been chatting to people for nearly fifty years.'

'Yes, but Tinder's a different beast.'

'Beast being the operative word,' I say, swiping a monster in a pink tuxedo to the left. I swipe a couple to the right on Tammy's insistence and eventually get another match.

'HI ARE YOU AN "A" LEVEL?' I have no idea what this means, so I just type a question mark. 'COS I'D DO YOU FOR 3 HOURS STRAIGHT'

'How do I block these losers?' I ask Tammy.

'I thought that was quite cute,' she says.

'You need help.' I say. Another match.

'WHAT DO YOU LIKE FOR BREAKFAST?' Niko asks.

'I usually skip breakfast,' I type.

'YOU'LL BE HUNGRY THEN. MAYBE I CUD BUY YOU DINNER?'

'Ooh, smooth,' Tammy says.

'He can't even spell *could*,' I say.

'You don't want him for his grammar,' Tammy says.

Another message says, 'SORRY, MAYBE I <u>COULD</u> BUY YOU DINNER?'

'See,' Tammy squeals. 'Message him back. Quickly.'

'Maybe you could,' I type.

'WANT TO SEND ME YOUR NUMBER?' he types.

Tammy squeals again, 'Quick, give him your number.'

'I'm not giving my number out to strangers on the internet.'

'You bloody well are,' she says, typing my number in and pressing send. My phone buzzes seconds later with a message from an unknown mobile.

'It's Niko. Meet me at the Italian Farmhouse at 7 Friday night?'

'Bit pushy, isn't he,' I say.

'Roberta,' Tammy warns me. 'You are going on a date. Let's find you something to wear.' She claps her hands excitedly. 'Ooh, a little black dress and killer heels.'

Chapter 4

#Karmakarmachickenshawarma

I haven't taken a selfie today due to having a chin full of spots. I updated my Facebook status with an old holiday photo to make it look like I'm having a great time somewhere hot and exotic. I'm officially a sad sack.

I received a weird email. It said: "He's your brother" in the subject line but wouldn't let me open the content. Bloody SPAM.

Karma didn't go well. I smiled at the girl in Greggs, and she thought I was a lezzer. I didn't dare ask for a slice of pie after that. I bought a cheese pasty, and it gave me heartburn, so creepy Nigel thought I was smiling at him. He came to sit with me in the canteen, and I had to listen to tales of cat wars, Marvel, and his demented mother. Not to mention having to watch him inhale his chicken shawarma. Note to self: Do not eat in the canteen again. Never, ever smile at the girl in Greggs. Tell Nigel I have some horrible, contagious disease, and he should stay well clear for a few years as it's a very long quarantine. Being kind is harder than it looks.

#funeralblues

I have to travel to Durham to sort out Mother's death certificate. We can't go and see her in the Chapel of Rest until we've produced it. It's procedure, apparently. I'm not even sure I want to see her in the Chapel of Rest, but Fliss insists I accompany her.

I avoid the quiet coach, in case I fall asleep. I sit alone, but I'm soon surrounded by a pack of Scotsmen returning from a stag weekend.

'Are ye no gonnae crack a smile, hen?' asks a large ginger man in a kilt with the Scottish flag painted on his face.

'You speaking English?' I ask.

'Ach, no, darlin', Ahm speaking Scottish. Wid ye like a swally?' He holds out a tin of cider.

'It's ten in the morning.'

'Is it? Jesus, I'm well behind. Best catch up quack.' He cracks open the cider and passes it to me, pulls open another, takes a big slurp, sits back and sighs.

So that is how I come to be steaming drunk on the train, singing football songs with a crowd of kilted men. I take a selfie of us all, then upload it to Facebook, Twitter and Instagram. It makes me look popular and a party animal. I'm awarded five "likes" immediately, and Dozy Darren from accounts has shared it. He needs to get a life.

I miss my Durham stop and have to get out at Darlington after swapping mobile numbers and saliva with Hamish McTavish who's actually from Glasgow. The taxi to Felicity's costs me seventy pounds and a headache on account of my cider withdrawal and the driver's love of Cliff Richard.

'You're drunk,' says my sister when she opens her door.

'Really?' I say. 'Hadn't noticed.'

'You're disgusting. Mother's not cold yet, and you're spending your inheritance and pissing it up the wall.'

'I wasn't aware there was an inheritance. Thought you'd have taken care of that.'

'What's that supposed to mean?'

'It means, sister dear, that you're a lying, stealing, no good…' I can't remember the rest, because I must have passed out.

I wake up shivering on the plastic sofa with Felicity's dog licking my face. At least someone in this house is friendly. I hear a man's voice from the kitchen, which jars my head. Note to self: If offered cider by steaming Scottish people, just say *no*.

'I understand you perfectly, Fliss. You're right, she can't just show up after all this time and expect to take over.'

'Who's taking over?' I croak from the couch.

'Oh, you're awake, then,' my sister says, sitting on the sofa with a cup of something hot.

'One of them for me?'

'If you get up and make it.'

I get up.

Her friend looks at her, and she shakes her head in a "don't ask" gesture.

'We haven't been introduced,' I say when I've made a cuppa and had a few slurps. 'I'm Roberta, Felicity's sister.' He takes my hand and shakes it, looking at Felicity for approval.

'I'm Gerard. Felicity has told me so much about you,' he says.

'I bet she has,' I say. 'She's never mentioned you.'

He titters nervously. 'I'm sorry to hear about your mother,' he says.

'It's ok,' I say.

'It's not ok,' Felicity shouts, jumps up, flounces out of the room and back into the kitchen. I hear her crying. He follows, and I hear him there-there-ing her. I retch and a bit of acid jumps into my mouth. I run to the sink and spit.

'For God's sake, Roberta, you're a bloody animal.'

#deaddrunk

I had ten pints of lager and a family-sized six pack of crisps last night. I slept in my clothes and wake feeling dirty (FYI grubby dirty, not sexy dirty). I delete the selfie I took due to having Hula Hoops crumbs on my chest. I update my Facebook with an old photo of me at the theatre.

It hasn't been a completely unsuccessful trip up to Durham. We manage to get the death certificate and produce it at the Chapel of Rest. They, then, allow us in to see a dead woman who doesn't look like Mother at all. Her hair is swept to the side in a fashion I've never seen her wear, and the make-up makes her look like an old tart. I try to tone it down a bit after Fliss bursts into tears and says she looks like a hooker. Her waxy face is as cold as a mossy river stone. I still feel nothing. Perhaps it will hit me at the funeral.

#olfactoryoddities

I update Facebook with a cryptic message about dating, then retweet one of my friend's posts about all men being bastards. Felicity messages me to say I'm mercenary and could I not wait until Mother is cold before I continue with my sordid love life. I resist the temptation to type, "Mother was always cold." I feel an odd sense of loss and emptiness and wonder how I could miss something I'd never really had. Maybe I'm grieving because there will never be a chance to mend our broken relationship. I remember the letters. Releasing them from the band, I sit on the bed and begin to read.

Letter number three:
30th November, 1940
Dear Michael,
I can't believe it's been so long since I saw you. It seems like yesterday, and it seems like a lifetime ago when I left the station.

Getting here was an operation. We were lined up along the roadside like soldiers. The streets were lined with sobbing and anxious mothers. Ours had stayed behind to look after you. I had a gas mask, a label pinned to my jacket and a bag holding my pyjamas, a change of underclothes and some sandwiches. I was alone. More alone than I've ever felt without you to keep me company.

Some of the lucky kids got sent to Canada and America. They were the posh ones, not us lot from East London. We were too rough and ready. The train journey was a bit bewildering, and when we got there, we were herded onto a big field, lined up, prodded and poked, checked for head lice and selected. It was like being at an auction. The least damaged goods were sold off first. A little girl next to me cried the whole time and promised to be good.

'Why are you promising to be good?' I asked.

'I must have been naughty to be sent away,' she said. I tried to explain what I understood to be happening, but she just howled louder.

When the Mister and Missus came, I tried to hide. They didn't have kind eyes or smiley mouths like some of the foster-parents. I prayed they wouldn't pick me. They felt my limbs, like you would check those of a horse you were buying at mart. They looked at my teeth. They were told they'd receive 8d a week for me, and they said they'd take me.

I was lifted onto a cart filled with hay, and we trundled for what seemed like miles through smelly countryside until we came to the farm. A giant dog, who looked like the devil, greeted us with growls and barks.

'Stay down, Satan,' the Mister said. 'It's just us.'

For the whole time I've been here, Satan eyes me hungrily, as if he'd like to tear me apart and devour me for his lunch. Hurry up and get here. Please.

Yours,

Alice

Dear Alice,

One night last week, I was lying in bed, and I heard a German bomber overhead. I limped into the street to see it. A hatch opened underneath it, and two bombs dropped into the graveyard over the road. You've never seen such a God Almighty mess. Rotting body parts and skeletons were scattered everywhere. The smell of death made me physically sick. Lucky I'm ill, or I'd have had to join the others in reburying the bodies. Archie McGinty has gone weird since then. His eyes are glazed over, and it's like there's no one home. He wanders the alleys, muttering to himself. Mr Winter says he's not the full shilling anymore.

Mrs Patterson has lost her babby. During the air raid, she handed him to a nun while she ran to pull little Tommy from under the collapsed counter of the store. They ended up in different shelters, and she hasn't been able to find her again. She wanders the streets with a lost look in her eye, crying the babby's name into the darkness, while the wardens try to drag her back into the shelter.

We were sitting in the street tonight, and I noticed a beautiful sunset. The horizon was alight with shades of red, orange and amber. A bittersweet sky. We marvelled at the spectacular sight until Mr Jones told us the colours were due to fires in the docklands. I waited with nausea for Father to come home, and when his familiar gait was a jaunty silhouette against the bloodshot sky and his boots crunched on the cobbles, I flung myself at him. 'Steady on, soldier,' he said. 'What's the matter with you?' I told him the docks had been bombed, and I was worried he wasn't coming back. He ruffled my hair and said, 'It'll take more than a few Germans to fettle me.' No new Meccano set for me. Thank God.

Your loving brother,
Michael

Letter number four:
15th November, 1940
Dear Michael,
We hear tell of bombs dropping and thousands of people being made homeless. We hear of camps in Epping Forest and on the platforms of the Tube stations. I imagine the dirt, the dust, the smoke, the smell of burning timber. I see homes sealed, windows blacked out, fires glaring, blazing orange. I see bomb-blasted gardens and leafless trees as though winter has come too soon. I see houses sliced in half as though cut with a giant knife. I see upstairs floors jutting out in mid-air, beds and wardrobes standing like tombstones. I see slivers of glass and shattered lives coated with dust and shrouded in death.

I hear the ack ack of shells and see buildings sandbagged against the tide of bombs. I see searchlights reaching with their fingers of light into the sky to pick out those planes. I see Mother and Father with dark circles round their eyes. I see the living dead walking the streets of London.

You have no sweets, no fruit, no toys, no comics. And still I wish I was there with you, instead of being here. Alone. With Them.
Yours,
Alice

I had to tear myself away from the letters to go to work. I hadn't realised that Mother had had such a hard time during the war. She never spoke of it. I intend to delve back into the past later tonight, but in the meantime, I have a date.

Chapter 5

I'm sitting in the Italian Farmhouse, drinking gin and bitter lemon and waiting for Niko to arrive. Tammy made me wear a strappy black dress and Karen Millen shoes, which are already cutting my feet in two. She'd decided I should have a safe word, in case he's a psychopath. My safe word would be any letter. At first, she said Bolognese, but I figured that if I was being murdered, I might not have the ability to type Bolognese, so we should use something simpler. I suggested a shorter word, and she suggested just a single letter and she'd come to the rescue. I sit at the table alone, and my phone beeps. A message from Tammy.

'Everything ok? Xxxxxxxxxx'

'Yes,' I type and press send. I feel guilty, so I type an X to represent a kiss.

'Is that a single letter because you're in trouble or a kiss?' Jesus wept.

'It was a kiss,' I type.

'Ok.'

'K,' I type. 'And that was me just saying ok, ok?'

'Ok.' I'm losing the will to live.

Niko arrives, dressed in Versace and smelling of something expensive and exotic. His hair looks wet, but as he kisses me on the cheek and hands me a daffodil, I feel the stickiness of the hair gel I thought had gone out of fashion with pedal pushers and winkle pickers. My cheek clags to his. I wipe mine with the back of my hand.

'Sorry I'm late,' he says.

I know you're thinking that this could be the start of something big. Something wild and romantic. Something that lasts a lifetime. Wrong.

The very first thing (and the last) Niko says to me is would I give him a rim job because I look like the kind of girl who'd enjoy it.

Taxi for one, please.

***

I get home and charge my phone. As soon as it starts up, my inbox is going crazy. I have three Tinder messages. One from Mark, who wants to know if I do anal. Another from Tim, who calls me *my dear* and asks if I believe in love at first "site". I'm not sure which site he means. Caravan site by the look of his string vest and tragic dye job.

The last is from Nigel who tells me: 'I CAME ACROSS YOUR PROFILE AND COULD NOT BELIEVE MY EYES. I HAVE TO TELL YOU HOW ENAMOURED I AM OF YOUR HEAVENLY BEAUTY. YOU ARE OBVIOUSLY INCREDIBLY ARTICULATE, INTELLIGENT, HUMOROUS, DILLIGENT AND PERCEPTIVE. PERHAPS WE TWO OBVIOUSLY WAGGISH INTELLECTUALS COULD WHILE AWAY MANY HOURS IN SCINTILLATING REPARTEE. AND WHEN THE BUDS OF OUR MUTUAL APPRECIATION AND PLATONIC ENGAGEMENT BLOSSOM INTO A CULMINATION OF RAMPANT SEXUAL DESIRES, THE STARS WILL GUIDE OUR LASCIVIOUS, LIBIDINOUS AND LECHEROUS DESIRES INTO AN ACT SO FULL OF LUSTFUL ABANDONMENT THAT WE WILL LOSE OUR LICENTIOUS SOULS FOREVER.'

I send back 'WTF?'

His reply is: 'DO YOU LIKE IT DOGGY STYLE?'

When I don't reply: 'CAN I AT LEAST DRY HUMP YOU?'

I finally find the BLOCK button.

#washout

I have had no time for bloody selfies today as the day has been a dead duck. The washing machine flooded the kitchen, and I spent all day wading through and mopping up water. I retire to bed exhausted with a Crunchie and a bottle of cabernet sauvignon. I make the mistake of tiptoeing through Tinderland, and I get a message from a guy who wants to take me out. Why not? I think.

I meet him in a pub in town, thinking I can escape to the toilet and leave out of the back door if he's a loser. He drinks his body weight in Sambuca, cries about his ex-wife, asks if he can suck my toes, then throws up in my cleavage while I wait with him for his taxi. The title "Loser" was made for this guy.

'You can't give up yet,' Tammy says when I call her to tell her I've had enough.

'One more,' I say. 'And if that's a disaster, that's it. The finish. The end. Finito. Nil morem saddo datio.'

#fiftyshadesofshit

I take today's selfie in bed. I'm eating. I have nothing else to do in bed after all.

I spend the day on hold to the insurance company's "speedy 24/7 helpline", only to be cut off when I eventually get through. I get another email from that same "no reply" address with the subject line: "Search and you shall find". It also won't let me open the content. It's probably a virus.

I retire to bed with *Fifty Shades*, fajitas, a case of Mojito, and a chocolate orange cream. I hit quite a few of my five a day there.

My next match on Tinder is none other than my ex-husband. Cheating bastard. 'Tammy, I can't do this anymore,' I say to her on FaceTime. She's waxing her top lip and has her hair in heated rollers. 'It's soul destroying.'

'I've had a little bit of success,' she says.

'When?' I ask. 'With who?'

She tears off the white strip and winces. 'Kevin was ok,' she says.

'Kevin,' I shriek. 'The one who brought the full-size Miss Piggy in his backpack and sang to her?'

'He was quite a nice kisser,' she says. 'And Marlon was ok until the cats.'

'Until the cats?' I squeal. 'He was a grade-A psycho. Asking you to make out in front of thirty pussies.'

'Yeah, that was a bit weird.'

'A bit?'

'There was Alan. He wasn't too bad.'

'He certainly wasn't husband or father material. I wouldn't trust him to look after a caterpillar. Didn't his mam put him on the bus?'

'Well, yes.' She pats her red lip with a tissue.

'And didn't he have the money for dinner in a marked envelope?'

'He did.' She sighs.

'Is that really all that's out there? It's enough to turn us gay,' I say.

'Don't you get any ideas,' she says. 'Just because I've got a 'tache doesn't mean I'm liking the beard.'

#facetiousfaeces

I take a selfie on the bus, which is full of plebs.

When I get to work, I'm called into the boss's office where I'm bollocked for being late. I try to explain that I'd caught the train instead of the bus, and the kids from the estate had nicked some of the lines to weigh them in at the scrap yard, but he won't listen. We had to wait an hour for a bus. When it turned up, it was a minibus. We were packed in so tightly, there was no room for a needle to be poked. I was practically on the knee of a fat man with fishy feet and sideburns. He kept thrusting his hips and winking at me. The woman to my right smelled of Brussels sprouts and bleach.

'It's just not good enough, Gallbreath,' he says. 'Punctuality's important.'

'So are train lines,' I say.

'Don't be facetious,' he says.

'Isn't that poo?' I ask.

'What?' he says, looking at me like I've eaten his firstborn. 'Get out of my office, Gallbreath. Consider this a verbal warning.'

'What if I get the train company to write a letter?'

'About what?'

'Never mind.' I've written it all down, though, so when I sue for constructive dismissal, I have the evidence.

That's another symptom I've noticed lately – I'm losing my mind.

I've always been a bit dizzy, in a female Mr Bean kind of way, but now, I'm positively senile. It's got to the point where I walk into rooms and forget why I'm there. I keep putting my car keys in the fridge and trying to open the Corsa door with a carrot. And when I've had alcohol, it's a thousand times worse.

Just the other week, I'd partaken of an alcoholic beverage or two with friends and colleagues (translates as got shit-faced with the girls and a couple of misfits from the office) and in the taxi home had given my address as 24, The Parkway. This is actually my former address, only I haven't lived there for fifteen years. It wouldn't be so bad, but my ex-husband still lives there with his partner and child. Imagine his consternation if I'd turned up at three in the morning and puked on his parquet. He was never into foreplay, so I reckon floor play would be out of the question too. I can't imagine Terri-Ann being impressed. She looks the type who only has alcohol when she visits someone in hospital and washes her hands on the way into the ward. I bet when they shag, she leaves her tights on. Mind you, it's the only way she'll get toe-curling sex with him. LMAO.

'I need Friday off, Mr Oldham,' I say.

'Sorry, no can do,' he says.

'It's my mother's funeral,' I say.

He sighs, running his hand through his thinning hair. 'Oh, for God's sake, that's most inconvenient.'

'I did tell her to hang on until the Wardle contract was complete, but she just selfishly closed her eyes and carked it.'

'Well, I trust you'll be back as soon as it's over?'

'Oh yeah, before they pick her out of the fire grate, I'll be tear-arseing it back to the office to make sure the paperclips are tidy.' He looks at me over his glasses and sighs again. I thought I was impassive, but the man has a swinging brick for a heart.

#analdiscourse

Allison is my intern. She's quite a few columns short of a spreadsheet (bless her). She calls me on the internal phone and says that Oldham wants me to do anal.

'Say what?'

'He just said to remind you you're doing an anal thing with him later.'

'I'm really not,' I say. 'You must've misheard.' Then, it dawns on me what she meant.

'You mean the oral presentation,' I say.

'Ah, yes, that's it.'

I say, 'If you don't know your oral from your anal, you're in trouble.' No wonder she walks funny.

***

I've been chatting to Dave for a few nights. He seemed ok, and by ok, I mean nice, intelligent, normal. That just shows how wrong you can be! He suggests we go out for drinks. He lives in Durham, so it seems like a good idea to meet in a pub in the city centre. I've just got parked and am headed to the Shakespeare, a small pub in which he'd suggested we meet, when he messages to say, 'Can we meet at mine, I'm running a little late.' He includes his address. It's right in the heart of the city centre, not the remote farmhouse location you might expect from a serial killer, so I figure I'll be safe.

I can tell it's a really small flat, so I'm surprised when he doesn't answer immediately. I knock for about five minutes. When he eventually comes to the door, I realise what's been keeping him. He opens the door and stands there, completely naked, with his hands full. Very full. The grunt, when it comes (pardon the pun), could have been heard three streets away.

'ARE YOU KIDDING ME?' I shout.

'Sorry, I was so excited that I was going to meet you in the flesh, I just couldn't help myself. I thought you might enjoy it,' he says to my back as I turn right round and speed off in the opposite direction. I don't even head for the gin bar. Straight to the car and home to block him and anyone who looks remotely like him.

Chapter 6

#gymnasty

I took a selfie of me on my bike and uploaded it to Facebook, Twitter and Instagram. I got no likes. What is wrong with people? Don't they realise what a problem exercise is when you're middle-aged and you've had a few kids. There are only certain things you can do without bladder leakage. Running's out, dancing's out, cycling makes you sore and not in a good way. After eight miles this morning, I felt like I'd had a gang bang with the Chippendales (not the Disney ones – I'm not some kind of pervert). There I was, pedalling down the high street wearing a luminous green, high-visibility jacket and orange helmet, while all the local kids pointed and laughed. Which was better than the return journey when they threw stones and called me Mr Bean and Mary Poppins. I should bloody well sue Victoria Pendleton.

Swimming's ok, if you don't mind being perved over by the wrinkly brigade, but the chlorine turns your hair green, which is not a good look. So, you see, I have a bevy of very good excuses why I can't shed those extra pounds.

I joined Lloyds today. It's full of posey types admiring their sculpted abs and bulging biceps in shiny mirrors. I feel like mashed potato and gravy in my black and tan Tesco ensemble.

As if I don't feel inadequate enough, the last thing I need to see is perfect Pamela leaning up against the water machine and fluttering her eyelashes at the attendant. She's size triple zero. The skin on her face is as tight as a nun's hymen, and she has bot cheeks like lychees. She must be the only person in the world who can make tangerine spandex look attractive. She's wearing a silver thong over the orange all-in-one. I can't help but think of cheese wire. She's got limbs like cocktail sticks. No saggy boobs from Princess Pamela. She uses her breasts to keep her chin warm. There's me in my tatty T-shirt with the mushy pea stain on the front and the brown iron mark on the back, the hairs on my legs poking through the Lycra of my leggings.

She's on the cross trainer. Only it doesn't look cross when she's on it. It looks downright bloody furious when I clamber aboard. I swear I can hear it wheeze when my size sevens start to pound its pelvic floor. It practically screams at me to get off after ten minutes, and a little pool of oil has collected on the ground beneath it.

I'm trying to keep my back to the wall so that sexy Steve with the pert pecs can't see my cellulite. I try and stick close to Bertha, who makes me look like Claudia Schiffer's prettier sister. She's got a face like a half-eaten trifle and legs like turkey and cranberry sarnies in cling film. Her feet smell of cheese, but she masks the eau de Camembert with lavender and ladybird antiperspirant.

Her Royal Perfectness has just done 365 chin-ups in forty seconds and is now practising her splits as Steve gives immoral support. I do ten sit-ups then disappear to the toilets, so they can't hear me wheezing. They're all taken, except the accessible one and I'm desperate. That's one of the reasons I hate my kids – that and the stretch marks. I only have to cough, and leakage occurs. If I sneeze, it's like a scene from *The Dambusters*.

I nip into the accessible bog. No one will mind. I didn't see anyone with a wheelchair in the gym. It's just political correctness gone mad. I pull down my kecks and sit myself down. Hot waterfall bliss. Only it's one of those dodgy seats with the big gap between the bit where your bum cheeks sit and the toilet bowl. I know nothing more until a warm stream runs down the back of my leggings and little tinkles of pee splash over my running shoes. You have got to be blooming well kidding me.

I pull up the soggy bottoms, open the door a slit and peep out. Luckily, Pam's not there. I creep out, my Hi-Tech trainers squelching and *splacking* on the tiled floor. A look behind me in the full-length mirror reveals the true horror. I sidle out of the door, wondering how I will get from the corridor to the car. Thank Christ I didn't come on the bus.

I pad down the hall and sneak through the outer door, just in time to face sexy Steve coming back the other way, arm in arm with perfect Pamela. His eyes fall to my crotch area and fill with horror. A smile slides across her face.

'Little accident, Roberta?' I resist the urge to smack her in the mouth, shove my nose in the air and march through the door, tripping over my sodden laces and falling headlong into a wall of clematis.

#men-o-pause

I tweet about going to the gym. Obviously leaving out the pee incident. I update my Facebook profile with a Photoshopped picture of me looking athletic. The work it took on screen to tone up those biceps is nobody's business. I accidentally take a selfie of my bottom when I sit on the phone in the doc's. I visit after work to receive medical confirmation that I might indeed be menopausal. The doctor asks me what I weigh.

'Dunno,' I say.

'Get on the scales,' he says.

'I really don't want to.'

'Roberta, get on the scales.'

I shake my head. He practically pushes me. I should report him to the GMC. He peers at the traitorous red line over the top of his glasses and types, "obese" on his desktop computer.

'Obese?' I almost scream.

'It's just according to your BMI,' he says.

'So, I'm not obese?'

'Well, you could do with losing a couple of pounds.'

You're not exactly ano-fucking-rexic yourself, I want to yell.

'So, what other symptoms have you been experiencing as well as the anger and irritability?'

'What anger and irritability?' I ask.

'You're obviously a little tense.'

A little tense? I want to bite off his nose and spit it back at him. And that's when he says those words. The words that strike fear in the heart of every woman. No, not Rugby World Cup (who wants to watch overweight men in shorts playing with funny-shaped balls?).

'I think perhaps it could be the menopause. Have you experienced hot flushes and night sweats?'

'No,' I lie. The truth is, at this very moment, I feel like someone has lit a bonfire underneath me. Most nights, I wake soaked in sweat from head to foot. It's like sleeping with a hot spring.

My life is over. I'm menopausal, obese and an orphan.

It's Mam's funeral tomorrow, so I'm travelling to Durham on the train. I'm not looking forward to it, but then, I suppose, no one looks forward to funerals. Except taphophiles.

Chapter 7

#noweddingsandafuneral

I take a few of Mam's letters to read on the train to Durham. It's strange to think of her speaking from beyond the grave. Not that she's in a grave, but you know what I mean.

Letter number five:
19th November, 1940
Dear Michael,
You've no idea what it's like here without you. The silence is deafening. When you're used to the hustle and bustle of London, it's deathly quiet. The cars and the buses, the trains and the rattle of the underground, the chatter of people down the market, the clitter-clatter of dishes, the shouts of the hawkers. I miss it all so much.

Here, I wake to the cock crowing at an ungodly hour. I wash in cold water and make breakfast for the family. The Mister is out by this time. He comes in ruddy and hungry, and woe betide me if I don't have his breakfast on the table. The Missus fetches a pail of fresh milk, and I have to pick out the grass. It's unnatural. What's wrong with milk in a bottle? It's warm, too, like fresh piss. She sees me gurn my face and says, 'Ooh, look at her majesty. What's the matter? We not good enough for ye?'

'No, Missus…I mean, yes, Missus.' I don't know what I mean, except I mean to stay pain-free without sore lugs. You've no idea how strong her arms are. A blow from her has my ears ringing like the bells of Bow.

Hurry up and get here.
Yours,
Alice

Dear Alice,
Tonight's bombing was a shower of slow-burning incendiaries. I sat on the crumbling porch of the store with a crocheted blanket wrapped round my knees watching everyone running around with buckets, smothering the flames with sand and earth. Cassie Moon bravely put out a fire on a man's roof by climbing up and using a bucket and a stirrup pump. I felt useless, sitting there with my dodgy lungs. As much use as a chocolate teapot, I am. I feel as low as a snake's belly. Everywhere there are posters about what we can do to do our bit. 'Keep on, London,' they tell us. 'Keep your chin up.' My chin's in the dirt and the dust and the rubble with the bones of the dead. The Mister and Missus surely can't be as cruel as the Germans' bombs. I think of you every day. I wish I was there, for you wouldn't want to be here.
Your loving brother,
Michael

Letter number six:
25th November, 1940
Dear Michael,
There's a dance in the village hall this coming Saturday. I was hoping you'd be here so that we could go together. The Missus says I'm too young for dances, but the Mister says everyone must go as it's a family dance.

They're saying here that the war will be over by Christmas, and I'll be able to move back to the Smoke. The ugly sisters say, 'Good riddance to bad rubbish.' Don't know who they're calling rubbish. They wouldn't say that if you were here.

Remember that time in school when Mr Barraclough was picking on me? He did it every lesson when I couldn't remember my seven times table. He'd whacked me with the strap four times already, and you'd just had enough. You jumped on his back to stop him whacking me again. You were given six of the best, and you laughed in his face as you were proud you'd stuck up for me.

When we got home, Father said he was proud of you, too, and Mother said she was ashamed that a son of hers had had the cane, but we could tell she was pleased, really.

I have to start a new school here on Monday. I'm dreading it. I imagine the teachers to be monsters and the children to be demons. Wish you were here. See you soon.

Yours,
Alice

Letter number seven:
6th December, 1940
Dear Michael,
School was just as torturous as I imagined it would be. The girls whispered and giggled behind their hands, and the boys threw stones at me and pulled my pigtails.

When we arrived, a tall girl rang a bell, and we were all shunted into lines. A master patrolled the lines to make sure we were standing straight and tall. He whacked our legs and arms with a cane until we were as tidy as he wanted us to be. We were then marched into our classrooms, and I was told to find a seat. There was only one vacant one at the front of the room, next to a boy with a shaven head, a back-to-front jumper and bare feet.

'Thomas Pye, how many times have I told you, you must wear shoes to school?' boomed a tall and loud woman in a flowered dress and lace-up shoes. 'Come out here.'

The poor boy slunk to the front of the room and held out his hand while she slapped it with a strap.

'He doesn't have shoes,' said a red-haired girl with a giggle.

'Then, he's to be pitied, is he not?' I said.

'Oh, hark at you, Miss Charity,' she said.

'Silence in my classroom,' the teacher shrieked, slamming a ruler down on the desk in front of me and nearly causing me to leave my skin behind. There followed a lesson on fractions where I was in trouble again when she asked what my share of the cake would be, and I answered none.

'Of course, it's not none,' she said.

'It is, Missus. If there's cake to be had in our house, I won't be getting none,' I said. She started going on about cheek and double negatives and cockney brats. I thought it best if I just stayed quiet, because you know what I'm like when I start with something, and you weren't here to jump on her back.

I can't believe I have to come here again tomorrow. It's worse than our school in London.

Yours,
Alice

Dear Alice,

I've had a bit of a relapse, and it doesn't look like I'll be coming after all this weekend. I can taste the disappointment. It has lumps in it. Last night was a heavy night of shelling. The sirens screamed, the anti-aircraft guns blazed as the planes dropped their bombs. I didn't have the energy to get to the shelter in time, so I watched it all from the church.

A small boy who I recognised to be one of the Wilsons ran across the street and into the church. He grabbed my arm and stared at me with horror in his eyes.

'What's wrong?' I asked. He couldn't even speak. He pointed in the direction of the Anderson shelter on the corner and dragged at my sleeve. When I got there, I realised the shelter had taken a direct hit, and the rest of his family were trapped inside. I started tearing at the rubble with my bare hands, but I couldn't move enough. They were going to suffocate inside.

My eyes cast around for something to use and miraculously a shovel lay in the debris of the school. I dug and dug like my life depended on it. But it was their lives that depended on it. People began to arrive and took over. I collapsed in a heap, wheezing, and the medic attended to me. I watched as they pulled Mr and Mrs Wilson and their twins from the rubble, their eyes red and glassy, their lungs rasping, coughing and retching, but they were alive and smiling. They called me a hero. The word warms my insides.

Mother called me a stupid boy for not getting to the shelter in time, but her eyes lit up with pride when they told her what I done. I'm not useless after all. Fate's a funny old thing, innit? If I'd made it to the shelter, I'd never have seen little Johnny, and if little Johnny Wilson had made it to the shelter, he'd have been buried alive with the rest of his family, and no one would have known they were there. No more chocolate teapot. I'm now a champ.

Your loving brother,
Michael

So, Mother had had a hard time at school just like me. I'm surprised, then, that she wasn't more sympathetic. Maybe she thought being kind would make me soft and the indignities would be worse to bear. I want to give her the benefit of the doubt. I want to believe she had my best interests at heart and that she wasn't just cold, callous and unloving.

The funeral goes as well as can be expected, considering my sister and I are in the same room for more than two hours. It's a humanist ceremony, which itself is ironic, because Mother wasn't a bit human. It's a small affair, on account of Mother going out of her way to piss off almost everyone she met. The bingo caller, Boris, is there, and Mr Vicky, who goes to all local funerals for a free feed. A couple of nurses from the hospital attend out of duty. I thank them for coming and assure them they don't have to try to find something nice to say about her as they search their brains for complimentary anecdotes.

'She was a character,' one of them manages. Ten out of ten for effort.

'She was that, alright,' I say.

Chapter 8

#treadsoftly

I sleep all day and don't want to get out of bed. I feel strangely depressed.

#ladieswhomunch

Tammy, in her wisdom, thought a trip to Tinderland might make me feel better. How wrong she was. Fifteen minutes in Louis's company was more than enough. He took a selfie of us at Costa, uploaded it to Facebook, changed his relationship status to "in a relationship" and tagged me in his photo as "The One". Ten minutes! Now I've blocked everyone whose name begins with L, and I've disappeared to the pub to meet the work crowd.

I take a group selfie in the pub and upload it to Facebook. I'm in the foreground, so my biceps look bigger than Mick the Dick's quads. I must remember to stand at the back in future or put my hands on my hips to disguise the bingo wings, like Tammy taught me.

'So, this article I was reading says you lose your libido,' I tell Tammy. I never in a million years thought I'd be swapping stories with anyone about mood changes, muffin tops, and moustaches.

'What's a sunbed got to do with it?' she asks.

'You are a thicket,' I say. 'It means you don't want to have sex. You have no sex drive.'

'That's news to me,' she says. 'Last I heard, you were gagging for it and had even contemplated shagging Dave.'

'Tammy, can we get one thing straight – in no circumstance, alive or dead, whether I was the last woman on Earth, he'd undergone a full body and face transplant and I was under the influence of chloroform would I ever consider sleeping with Dave. He's worse than Mick the Dick. And I don't mean it's happened to me yet. But this article is about the things nobody tells you about the menopause. Loss of libido means the loss of your sex drive. It's one of the symptoms, losing your mojo.'

'Ah, right, but *you* haven't?'

'No. But I might.'

'So, we're still trying to find a victim. While you've still got it, I mean. Your lido.'

'That makes me sound like a praying mantis in a paddling pool.'

'A conquest, then?' she says. 'That reminds me – William from HR with the big nose has been asking after you. Think he's got the hots. Mick said you were taken.'

'What did he do that for? I quite like William the Conk.'

'Cos he's a miserable sod, and he doesn't want anyone else to be happy?'

As if summoned by our conversation, Mick wanders over pretending to be nonchalant. 'You ladies going out to lunch today?'

'I'm nipping to Greggs,' Tammy says. Great – now we sound like skanks, and Mick will look down his nose at us.

'Actually, I was thinking of going to Jamie Oliver's,' I say.

'Were you?' Tammy says. 'You never mentioned it. I thought you wanted me to get you a pie from Greggs cos the serving girl thinks you fancy her.' I kick her twice during this little spiel, and still, she doesn't get the hint. Frickin' moron.

'So, we're holidaying in Lesbos this year,' Mick says.

'You're such a pig,' I say.

'Ooh, I love it when you talk dirty. Me and some of the lads are going for a drink after work, if you fancy joining us.'

'I'd rather swim with stingrays,' I say.

'Yes, alright,' Tammy says at exactly the same time.

'Good, I'll see you in the Dog and Gun about six,' he says. Great, now, I won't be able to relax. I never can in Mick's company. Maybe because I'm secretly attracted to him. There's no way anyone's going to know that, though. Not even Tammy. Especially not Tammy. Mick is not relationship material and is best avoided.

As often happens at moments like this, I subconsciously picture Mick and me in bed. He kisses me softly and whispers how gorgeous he thinks I am. Lies. All lies. He can't wait to get away from me the next day.

A flush comes from my boots and burns my face.

'Geez, Bob, you've lit up like a Belisha beacon.' He's been calling me Bob since the first time we met. I was working on a new contract, and he TUPE'd over from Madleson-Ferris and Wolf. He called me Robbie, and when I asked him not to call me that, as I didn't like shortened versions of my name, he decided to be even more annoying and shorten it to Bob.

'So, Dog and Gun?' Mick asks.

'Yes,' Tammy says. 'We'll be there.'

'What did you have to do that for?' I ask her when he's gone.

'Jonathon from accounts is going with them.'

'Jonathon?'

'The sexy new lad with the blond surfer hair and tattooed sleeve.'

'Jesus, Tam. I've got bras older than him. I have a rule: if I could've given birth to it, I don't shag it.'

'Not for you, for me,' she says.
'You're the same age as me.'
'Yeah, but I look younger.'
'Cheeky bitch.'

***

So here we are, in a dingy pub, with Jonathon from accounts (hereafter known as the Foetus), Mick the Dick, Nigel, and a gaggle of giggling twenty-something girls.

'My dinner had a bigger IQ than most of these,' Mick says, sidling up to me gripping a cocktail in his greasy paw. I'm annoyed at the excitement rising inside me. I feel a flutter in my chest, and my legs turn cold and feel weak. I hate myself for wanting to be kissed by him.

As you may be aware by now, Mick and I have history. It's no great romance, like *Gone with the Wind* or *Wuthering Heights*. More Bad with the Wind and Withering Tights.

It happened at a two-day conference in Harrogate. I stayed at the Swan, and he did a bit of ducking and diving. Before I knew it, I was in his room on the pretence of having coffee (such a bloody cliché). I was vulnerable. My boyfriend at the time had been bonking Barbara from the prize bingo.

Mick told a couple of jokes during dinner, and in my cocktail-induced reverie, I might have cracked a smile, so he thought his luck was in. Turns out, it was. His luck. In. Only because I'd drunk three litres of tequila, and with every pint, he got better looking. By the fourth pitcher, I'd have humped the Bee Gees.

We fell into his hotel room doorway, ripping off each other's clothes and panting. The next thing I remember is waking up next to him and panicking. I threw on my crumpled clothes, glanced in the mirror and left before he could surface. He spent the whole day at the conference avoiding eye contact. I skipped lunch, even though I was starving, just so I didn't have to bump into him in the queue. You could have stirred the tension with a shitty stick. I left the conference early that afternoon on the pretence I'd had a call to say my house had been burgled.

When he was transferred to our department, he took great pleasure in being obnoxious to me and making me squirm every chance he got.

I pretended, of course, that I couldn't care less, but it was a bit hurtful. I mean, we had shared bodily fluids. They reckon you only regret the things you don't do, but that's rubbish. I've been regretting that night ever since. Now, he thinks he has one over on me.

'What did you have?' I ask Mick about his meal.

'Eh?'

'For dinner. You said these girls have a lower IQ than your dinner. What did you have? It makes a difference. A chicken has a lower IQ than a cow and a pig…'

'I had cabbage,' he says.

'That is an insult.'

'It's the truth,' he says.

'I'm flattered.'

'Why?'

'Well, you've come to sit with me,' I say.

'I thought you'd be missing me,' says Mick.

'I didn't try to hit you.'

'Very droll. You still got a date for the company ball?' he asks.

'Of course,' I lie. 'In fact, I have to dash right now, as I have a very hot date.'

***

It becomes apparent my "hot" date really isn't. He turns up on a motorbike, man-mountain size like the Hulk, carrying a spare helmet for me. I've just spent two hours in the hairdressers having a cut and blow dry, so I'm not best pleased.

He speeds around town like a jerk and then pulls up outside McDonald's. I hate McDonald's, and I hate the fact that he orders for me. Two large fries, two Big Macs and two Cokes. When we sit in a booth, he asks me why I didn't order anything. It transpires both meals are for him. When he drops me off, he asks for petrol money. When I refuse, he screams at me that I'm a tight bitch. Chivalry isn't dead yet. I check his Facebook status later, and he's written that he checked out tonight's date in Boots' window as she was riding pillion, and she looked chunky. Cheeky bastard!

Chapter 9

#midwifecrisis

Today's selfie is of me, my eldest, Shoni, and her Essex boy (actually he's not from Essex, but he should be. If you saw his teeth and ridiculous hairstyle, you'd get me). I upload it to Facebook, Twitter and Instagram after making myself look thinner and younger with the use of filters and Photoshop. I get twenty-four likes and three comments within minutes. One of the comments is from Mick: 'Looking good, kid.' Sarcastic twat. And what's with the *kid*? How patronising.

***

Don't ask about Shoni's name. Knobhead picked it. I'm sure he named her after an ex-girlfriend, but I could never prove it. I wanted to call her Miranda, but he vetoed that. He vetoed all my ideas. She's living with a drug dealer in Dagenham. She wanted to know if they could come and stay at mine for the weekend, as she had something to tell me. Please, God, don't let it be that she's pregnant, I thought. I can't be a granny on top of the mid-life crisis.

According to Shoni, I've been having a mid-life crisis for years. That's the pot calling the kettle grimy-arse. She was one of those teenagers who refused to eat meat or wear leather and wanted to divorce her parents because we smoked in the house. She said we were contravening her human rights by making her breathe our smoke, and she was going to seek legal advice. Turns out her friend's father was a lawyer, but he doesn't do pro bono work. (When I explained all this to Tammy, she thought pro bono was something to do with foreplay). I said Shoni contravened *our* human rights by making us listen to her bullshit. She wasn't amused.

She spent many a night in her bedroom dyeing her hair black, listening to seventies rock bands and pretending to self-harm. She wouldn't slash a bicycle tyre, let alone her own wrists.

Her father, of course, blamed me. Apparently, I'd spoiled her by allowing her freedom of speech and an opinion. A girl with an opinion? Where will it all end?

His opinion ceased to matter when he took up with Terri-Ann from Thomas Cook. I didn't see it coming, even though I'd found dinner receipts for two, and he'd started wearing Kouros again.

It got a bit messy because we fought over who would have the kids.

'I don't want 'em,' he said.

'Well, I'm not having them.'

'The woman always gets awarded custody.'

'Not these days,' I warned him smugly.

He wanted to relax in his clean apartment with Terri-Ann from Thomas Cook, who I saw in Ann Summers buying a butt plug. Tempted to tell her they come in extra-large, I resisted and left the shop feeling violated. I made sure the kids went over that night and warned them not to touch anything that looked like a bottle stopper.

The upshot was that Shoni was at the station, and could I pick her up? So, she wasn't really ringing to *ask* if she could stay. The car was being moody again, so I had to get a taxi.

Sonny from Krazy Kabs arrived. I hate it when Sonny picks me up. He always recounts in minute detail everything I said and did when drunk the weekend before. He's one of those who enjoys watching you cringe. A plaque on the door of his cab reads, "Your comfort is my business". It should read, "Your discomfort is my pleasure".

'Where to?' he asked.

'Train station please. I'm picking up my daughter.'

'You wan' me to wait?'

'Em, yeah, otherwise, we'll have to walk home again.'

'Exercise will do you good,' he said. 'Your daughter a fat bird too?' Now, he was really cruising.

'Now, listen, sunshine, I know some things get lost in translation, but you're really pushing your luck.'

'My lock. I do not know this.'

'Yeah, course ya don't. Just drive.'

When Shoni alighted from the carriage (carrying the bags, I might add, while the Dickhead from Dagenham waltzed off the train with his hands in his pockets), she looked two stone lighter, and her roots were showing.

'You're not pregnant, then?' I said, motioning to her flat stomach.

'No, I'm not bloody pregnant. Nice to see you as well, Mother.'

Dagenham smirked.

'Just asking. I thought that's what you might be going to tell me.'

'No,' she said, tight-lipped and sour-faced. 'Do you have to spoil everything, Mother?'

'What do you mean, spoil everything? I haven't done anything.'

'We wanted to tell you over dinner.'

'You've not won the lottery?'

'No, I haven't won the bloody lottery. We're getting married.'

'Oh,' I said. Well, what else is there to say? My eldest daughter thinks it's a good idea to shackle herself to a southern druggie and waster. Surely, she didn't expect congratulations.

'Oh?' she said. 'Is that all you can say? I thought even you might have managed to congratulate us.'

It seemed she did expect congratulations.

'What do you mean, *even* me?'

'Kevin, I told you this was a mistake. Let's just get back on the train.' She made to walk towards a train standing on Platform 1.

'That's going to Edinburgh,' I said.

'Piss off, Mother,' she said.

The cab ride home was silent and sombre, punctuated only with Sonny's boring banter.

'You are much thinner than your mother.'

'Yes,' Shoni said spitefully.

'You have your father's genes?'

'Probably,' she said. Traitor.

'Thought so,' he said.

I slammed the door on the way out and left Dagenham to pay the fare. I'm sure he'd have made enough profit in his latest cocaine haul.

When I wasn't menopausal, all of these things would have gone over my head, but now, I raged inside.

I dried the cutlery that was on my draining board, flinging those with water stains back into the sink. The clatter brought Shoni into the kitchen, eyes wide and questioning.

'Are you having a mid-life crisis, Mother?'

'I should think it's about fucking time for one,' I said. 'I'm sure I've earned it.'

'I thought we could go shopping…for the dress… I'd like you to come with me. Obviously, Kevin can't come, and my girlfriends will probably pick out ones that don't suit me. You're good at that kind of thing.'

'Who's paying for it?' I asked.

'Well, I thought that… I mean, we discussed before…'

'Me?'

'It's customary for the bride's parents to foot the bill,' said Dagenham, creeping up behind her.

I ignored him and turned to Shoni. 'So, what's Dickh… your father paying for?'

'Things are a bit tight at the minute…what with the little one…'

'You mean Terri-Ann from Thomas Cook is a bit tight. Well, he can pay his fair share. Right. Right?'

'Yes, Mother, I'll make sure he pays his fair share.'

'Ok, wedding dress shopping tomorrow. I can look for a mother of the bride outfit.' I started to get excited.

Big mistake.

Of course, it was not going to go well. Me, Shoni and a room full of meringues. It was a recipe for disaster.

#manicmeringues

Today's selfie was taken in the changing rooms. I'm wearing a MOB outfit and a hat that looks like a giant cupcake (BTW, MOB stands for mother of the bride, not mafia). I upload it to Facebook and get forty-three likes, so I Snapchat it to Tammy, and she sends me a pic back of her looking radiant surrounded by daisies. The Twitter pic gets fourteen love hearts and two shares.

The ride back to the station after wedding dress shopping is even more sombre and silent. Sonny has had an allergic reaction to cucumber (I didn't ask what he was doing with it) and has ended up in A and E with a swollen tongue (divine retribution), so his sidekick is taking us, and he doesn't speak a word of English.

Wedding dress shopping was a bit of a debacle. Of course, I'm getting the blame. I wasn't to know when she said, 'I want your honest opinion', she didn't mean she wanted my honest opinion. People should say what they mean. The mermaid one *did* look more like a demented trout. I was just being honest. The sparkly one *was* a bit 'Big Fat Gypsy'. If she didn't want my honest opinion, why ask for it?

'Tact, Mother,' she said. 'Diplomacy.' Note to self for next time: just say, 'That's nice', and smile.

'Would it have killed you to be nice for one day?' Shoni says in the cab. I have no idea what she's talking about. I can't help being honest. There's nothing wrong with honesty. There's little enough of it about. She should be grateful.

'Grateful?' she shrieks, pulling her luggage from the boot when I tell her as much. 'Grateful for you murdering my self-esteem, stamping on my dreams, butchering my shot at happiness.' Ever the drama queen. 'I bet you wouldn't have been like this with Carolyn.' Oh, here we go. 'Carolyn can do no wrong. I bet you wouldn't have said Carolyn's dress looked like dried-up seaweed.' She storms to the platform, and I have to run to catch up.

'I don't think those were my exact words,' I say. I've never been so bloody grateful to see a train.

Carolyn is my youngest. Shoni always maintains she's the favourite, which is inaccurate, cos I can't fucking stand any of them.

To top off my terrible day, tonight's date shows me a pair of sunglasses he shoplifted from a stall in the Metro Centre while we wait for a table at TGI Fridays. I nip to the loo and come straight home.

I should just say I can't make the company ball, and then, I won't need to put myself through this torture.

Chapter 10

#bellissimo

At work, Tammy and I decide to substitute the word bellend with *bellisimo*. We can now get away with inappropriate language, and people will think they're being complimented and not insulted. It's genius.

Today is just dire. Oldham's in a foul mood. Rumour has it, his wife has run off to Krakow with a Polish refugee. Mick says he knows this is a lie as he saw her in Sainsbury's this morning, and she wasn't even buying kielbasa.

'Maybe that's why he's in a mood,' I say, 'because she hasn't run off with a Polish refugee.'

'Have you seen his wife?' says Mick. 'Believe me, no one would run off with her. Eddie Hall would struggle to lift her off the ground.'

'Don't be sexist. Why is it a woman has to be beautiful and slim to be considered desirable? We have other qualities, you know.'

'I know, some of you can iron and cook,' he says, winking at Tammy.

'Men think they're God's gift, even when they're fat and bald, but if we so much as gain a few pounds…'

'A few,' he says, looking me up and down.

'Fuck off,' I shout, and storm from the office.

'Touchy,' I hear Mick say as I leave. I want to punch him repeatedly in the head until his brains seep out of his ears. I have no idea why, but tears prick the back of my eyes.

***

'You alright?' Tammy says when she finds me in the canteen later. 'Ignore Mick, he's a–'

'Bellissimo,' I say.

'Exactly, she says. 'I dunno why you let him get to you.'

'Neither do I.'

'It's not like you *like* him.'

'Can't stand him.'

'Or value his opinion.'

'God, no.'

'Then, why don't you just ignore him?'

'I will,' I say.

So next time he speaks to me, that's exactly what I do. Only he thinks it's hilarious.

'Sent me to Coventry?' he says. 'Ooh, I've really touched a nerve, haven't I? Maybe you should join Fat Fighters, if you're so touchy about it.' I still manage to pay no attention to him, though my blood's boiling at this point. 'I hear Lloyds have a pretty good gym. Pamela goes. Do you know Pamela? Gorgeous girl. Body to die for.'

'Well, go and die, then.' Damn – why can't I just ignore him? He practically skips down the corridor, and I imagine blowing poison darts at his back. I know why I can't just disregard him. I'm hurt. I like him more that I would ever admit to anyone. I'd let my guard down and slept with him, and now, I'm just another notch on his bedpost. I hate that. I'm angry at myself, and therefore, I'm angry with him.

I must get a date for the company ball and put him in his place once and for all. I spend the night trawling Tinder and talking to a number of eHarmony rejects. Frederick's an Elvis impersonator who lives with his granny and can't come on a date in Durham because a girl in Shotton Hall has a restraining order against him. Alrighty, then, let's speak… er…never. Guy is a Gandhi lookalike who states his "likes" as collecting carrier bags and fly fishing in Folkestone. I can just imagine Mick's comments if I turn up with someone like him.

'Tinder is evil,' I tell Tammy. 'I am never listening to you again about dating.'

'There's a speed dating night at Wetherspoon's tonight,' she says. 'Let's go. Just this once.'

'No,' I say. 'Absolutely not. I mean it. Never again. Nope. Nein. Non. Nah. Not in a million.' But I need a date for the company ball. I need to take someone who Mick can't deride or show disdain at. I need to look like I don't care about him.

***

We're parked on bar stools in Wetherspoon's. Little tables are dotted around with a chair either side. A man with grey hair and sideburns is holding a stopwatch and a bell. We're given numbers and allocated tables at which to start.

'Isn't it exciting,' Tammy says.

'About as exciting as dipping my fingernails in petrol and setting them on fire,' I say.

'Come on, Roberta, play the game.'

'I've been playing the game. It's called Frauds, Fruitcakes and Flakes.'

'It's three minutes of your life,' she says.

'Yes, ten times.'

'You might meet Mr Right.'

'And I might meet Mr Self-Righteous and Mr Look What I've Got in My Right Hand?'

'You're so negative,' she says. 'Put your name badge on and take your seat at table number one. When the bell goes, you don't do anything. The men will come to you. Here's your card. Remember to tick all those you want to see again.'

The whole process is as painful as kidney stones.

Mark sits in front of me and asks me how old I think he is.

'I don't know, how old are you?'

'Guess,' he says. Oh great, a three-minute guessing game, ffs.

''Bout forty,' I say.

'Thirty-nine,' he says. 'No one ever guesses right.' *Kill me now.*

'I could be watching *The Chase*,' I say in an aside to Tammy. 'Or even better, waxing my bikini line.' A bell rings, and the throng moves, and people take a seat at their next table.

Joe sits opposite me. 'I'm Joe,' he says. 'And you are?' *Read the freaking name badge, stupid.*

'Roberta,' I say.

'Tell me something interesting about yourself, Roberta,' he says.

'I crossed the Atlantic with Amelia Earhart.'

'Really,' he says. 'That's amazing.' *What a tit.*

'Tell me something interesting about you.'

'I make drawing pins,' he says. *Great, give me some to stick in my eyes. Ding, ding. Saved by the bell.*

Rick is next. He takes hold of my hand and kisses it before sitting down. I imagine he thinks it makes him seem charming when, really, it just makes him seem creepy. 'What would you like for breakfast?' he asks and then snorts at his "joke".

'Arsenic,' I say. 'Death will be a relief compared to this.'

'Oh, you're not a Debbie Downer, are you? I like to keep things positive.' Right now, I'd like to see a positive charge running from his testicles to his toes, preferably on the end of a rudimentary instrument of torture used in wartime by the Japanese army.

'No, I'm a Roberta Realist. I like to keep things real.'

'I'm hoping for lots of interest tonight,' he says.

'I wouldn't be too hopeful,' I say. 'I think you might be like Simon Cowell's dogs.' He looks confused. 'No ticks,' I tell him. The bell rings again.

Todd takes his spot at my table. 'It bodes well for me that you're impressed by speed,' he says, then laughs.

'Did you use that line on every girl in the room?' I ask, stifling a yawn.

'He used it on me,' the girl at table ten says. 'Wasn't funny, then, either.' I see him change the tick he'd put next to her name into a cross.

'You don't have a sense of humour?' he asks.

'Would I be here if I didn't?

'Do you always answer a question with another question?'

'Has it been three minutes yet?' *Ding, ding.*

Boris wants to know my plans for the future.

'To make it through tonight without throwing myself from a very tall building.'

'In five years' time, I see myself as being the owner of twenty-four cats,' he says. 'I want one Siamese, two long-haired Persians, a Cornish Rex, three Tonkinese, a British short hair, an Abyssinian, two Burmese, a Bengal, a Siberian, a Sphynx, five Russian Blue, a Himalayan, a Turkish Angora and three Chartreux,' he says. 'I'm going to call them Hughey, Alice, Terri, Trevor, Lulu, Don Estelle, Elton, Sammy, Cheryl, Simon, Susan Boyle, Grindl, Gracie, Kelly, Diana, Beatrix, Eugenie, Diversity, Pumpernickle, Peppermint Paddy, Peanuts, Jellybean, Jim and Brady.'

'How many cats do you have currently?' I ask.

'None,' he says. 'I'm in rented accomo, and the landlord is ailurophobic.'

'I hate cats too,' I say, beginning to hate Boris.

Ding, ding.

The next one is the worst. I don't even get a look at his name badge or his teddy boy haircut before he lunges at me with his tongue. Bilal, "Call me Billy", seems to think sticking his furry tongue in my gob is the way to get ticked. I want to tell him it's the way to get twatted.

The last one (thank the Lord), Bob (or Baab, as he calls himself in his fake American accent), wears satanic goat-head jewellery, has a tattoo of the Pope being shot on his wrist and is wearing a girdle. The only reason I'm aware of the girdle is because he's developed an itch and doesn't stop scratching for the whole three minutes. He calls me "dude", asks me if I like surfing and says he could really use a BJ.

'You could really use a personality,' I say.

Ding, ding.

***

Afterwards, we're supposed to mingle at the bar and exchange email addresses or bodily fluids with those people we've ticked. Even Tammy's sheet looks like a game of noughts and crosses.

'I gave them marks out of ten,' she says. 'There wasn't even a solid seven between them.'

'There wasn't even a solid seven with them all added together.'

'Let's get out of here,' she says. 'We can go to the Fighting Cocks in Durham and have a dance and a laugh.'

It turns out to be more a pint and a fight night, so we give up and get a taxi home.

'Just to confirm, Tammy, we are never going speed dating again.'

'I think it was the venue,' she says. 'Next time, we should go to a more upmarket one.'

'No, no, no,' I say. 'There is not going to be a next time. 'Tinder is bad enough, but that was excruciating.'

'It was a little rough,' she admits. 'Where the hell did they find those guys? One of them told me he fell off a boat onto a dead seal while fishing for mackerel in Northumberland. The seal was so decomposed, he was covered in rotting flesh, and the fisherman had to fish him out. Then, he told me he invented the story to impress me.'

'Dear God, we've had a lucky escape.'

Chapter 11

#ex-rated

I didn't take a selfie today, but I found a photobooth photo of me and an ex-boyfriend in the 80s. I Snapchat it to Tammy, and she turns us into dogs. When I get home, there's an answerphone message from Shoni saying she'll forgive me if I apologise. Sod that. There's also a Facebook message from my first serious boyfriend, Harry McGarrigle, asking if I'm *that* Roberta Gallbreath. If by *that* Roberta Gallbreath, he means the one he tried to grope in the bus stop outside the chippy and then cheated on with her friend when she was on holiday in Oban, then, yes, she is indeed *that* Roberta Gallbreath. He's sent a Facebook friend request, and I hum and ha about accepting. I press accept. I can always block him if he becomes a nuisance. He was quite good-looking in his day. He's probably as bald as a coot now and as round as the Coliseum.

His profile pic shows a distinguished-looking gentleman in a grey suit. His occupation is listed as CEO. Ooh, he's gone up in the world. He used to be a brickie's labourer. I message him:

'Yes, it is *that* Roberta Gallbreath. How are you?'

'Mustn't grumble. Lovely to be back in touch after all these years. We did have some fun, didn't we?'

If fun constitutes sperm in your hair and a quickie in a Cortina, then maybe, I think.

'We did,' I write, remembering my promise to myself to be nice.

'Would be lovely to meet up again,' he writes. *No, it bloody wouldn't*, I think. *Be nice.*

'It would be.'

'How about Thursday?'

'Great.' I can always make an excuse… I have toenails to pick or a toilet bowl to bleach.

'Café Rouge?'

'Sounds good.'

'Gotta dash. Fax to send before close of play.'

"Play" brings back memories of his teenage bedroom. Porn mags, potato wedges and out of date prophylactics.

Bugger, why did I have to add him? It would have been kinder to ignore him. Bloody Karma.

#hotflush

I have another answerphone message from Shoni accusing me of being immature and heartless, plus one from Carolyn condemning me for upsetting her sister. I don't know why she had to get involved; they can't bloody stand each other. They always seem to become great allies when they can gang up on me. Drew calls to ask if I can lend him five thousand.

'Five grand? For what?' Skunk is the first thing that comes to mind.

'I want to buy a burger van,' he says. 'It's a little gold mine. I could really make a go of a business with it.'

'I don't have five thousand to waste,' I say.

'It wouldn't be a waste, it'll be an investment.'

'I'll stick with premium bonds, thanks.'

'Thanks for the vote of confidence, Mother.'

He'd probably sell it the first time he was skint and couldn't be bothered to go to work. Then, he'd buy drugs and drink with the proceeds. I bite my tongue. Again.

It makes me feel like I'm going to explode. Being nice is overrated.

***

Hot flushes have me wafting bits of paper in a meeting and getting daggers from Oldham. If he was the one melting, he'd have turned up the air con until we had icicles hanging from our extremities. Selfish, insensitive creep.

'Turn that heating up,' he says when the clients have gone. 'It's bloody Baltic in here.'

'With respect, sir.'

'Gallbreath, you wouldn't know what respect was if it jumped up and bit you on the–'

'Sir, I don't think–'

'That's exactly right, you don't think. Making all that noise in front of the Carters.'

'That's not really fair…'

'Neither's the bloody weather. Now get back to work. We need this contract. Or do you fancy the TUPE over to Madarins? The managers there are bastards.' I can't imagine such a transfer rendering our employment terms any worse. These buggers want sinew from stones, never mind blood.

'And you're so liberal, so kind and considerate, such an all-encompassing joy to work for,' I say.

'Don't be funny, it doesn't suit you.' I catch sight of Mick smirking as I leave the office. Moron.

When I get home, there's a message from Harry reminding me about 'Our date lol.'

I message him to say, 'It isn't a date lol.'

He lols me again and then says he's G2G as he's chairing a meeting of the board.

Meeting of the bored, maybe.

I might just invite him to the company dinner dance. That would show Mick. After all, he's the CEO of a company. Tammy says that could mean anything. Trust her to pee on my parade. She says he's probably a plumber with two Polish skivvies working for him for fifty pence an hour. At least he's not a milk monitor (I'm showing my age. I know they don't have milk monitors anymore. Another of Margaret Thatcher's legacies. Why shouldn't people buy their own milk? If their kids have rickets, they've only themselves to blame).

Drew texts to say his dole has been stopped and could he borrow a fifty for essentials. I know essentials to be tobacco and beer, so I text I'll drop him some groceries round later and put some credit on his electric card.

'Don't bother,' is his reply, so I take it the essentials aren't. *Get on your bike*, I think.

***

That night I'm lying in bed and Dave number two messages on Tinder to say, 'YOU'RE STILL A HOTTIE, ROBERTA.'

'Thanks,' I send.

'WANNA GO OUT?'

The last thing I want to do is reapply my make-up, get dressed again and stagger about in heels for three hours, but the alternative is a party-political broadcast by the snowflake party or *Hetty Wainthropp Investigates*.

'Where to?' I ask.

'SOMEWHERE FOR A BITE?'

I hope he means we'll go for something to eat, and it isn't a kinky vampire fetish he's suggesting. You never know with internet dating.

'TGI Fridays in The Gate?' I type.

'PERFECT' he says. It isn't followed up with *WEAR SOMETHING SLUTTY* or *I COULD USE A BJ*, so things are definitely looking up.

It takes me half an hour to do my make-up, tease my hair into something that doesn't resemble bad bed head and throw on a black top and jeans with a denim jacket. I choose heels over flats and feel that familiar anticipatory feeling one gets before a date. That feeling that something wonderful could happen. That you might meet your soulmate. That this could be the first day of your happy ever after.

When I arrive at the Gate, he is already sitting in a booth in TGI Friday's. I hope he'll stand up to greet me. Then, I realise he is standing up. The six-two he'd detailed on his profile must've alluded to inches not feet. I could put him in my pocket. The profile picture must be at least ten years out of date too. Be polite, I tell myself. Do not call him a hobbit. Worse still, as I tower over him I notice he's beginning to go bald and has coloured in his bald patch with what looks like eyebrow pencil.

'Do you like birds?' he asks.

'Birds?' He isn't angling for a threesome already, surely?

'The feathered kind. I have budgies and canaries.' So, he isn't leading into a joke about a cockatoo. 'They make a bit of mess, and they can be noisy at breakfast time. Just thought I'd better warn you.' Easy there, tiger, let's get dinner over before we think about breakfast.

'I love your shoes,' he says. 'I love high heels.' Please tell me he doesn't mean wearing them.

'They kill your ankles, though,' I say. 'Not to mention your back.'

'I wouldn't know,' he says. Relief floods through me. 'They look gorgeous, though.' Phew, he's not a weirdo.

We order the food, and he asks to see my shoes again. 'May I?' he asks, touching the heel. 'Beautiful.'

'Are you in the fashion industry?' I ask him – he seems unusually preoccupied with my footwear.

'No, I work at Hartlepool docks. We make undersea cables for the offshore industry. Wind farms and the like. It's all a bit boring, really. May I?' he asks again, nodding towards my heels.

'You don't want to try them on, do you?' I ask.

'Hahaha, no,' he says. 'I'm not a transvestite.'

'Can't say I'm not relieved. Not that I'd judge.' He strokes the leather of my eBay purchased Louboutins (from the USA, eighty pounds, and they were still in the box), a look of bliss crossing his face.

'I'm so pleased you're not the judgemental type,' he says. 'Those soles are to die for.'

'Yes, they're my favourite shoes,' I say.

'Do you have photos of any others?' Ok, things are beginning to enter the realms of the creepy. He starts to shake. He closes his eyes and breathes heavily.

'Are you ok?' I ask.

'Yes. It's just…'

'What?'

'I wanted to ask you something.'

'Yes?'

'Please may I lick them?'

'Eh?'

'Your shoes. I just want to lick them.'

'No, you bloody cannot.' I stand to leave. He "accidentally" drops his fork on the floor and crawls under the table to pick it up. As I try to barge past him, he licks the heels and soles of my shoes. I run all the way home and stay in a steaming shower for forty-five minutes. What is wrong with these people? I'll watch *Hetty Wainthropp* on Catch Up. It'll remind me of all the other evil in the world. Like appalling TV.

#French

I sweat so much through the night, I wake up with a hangover, and I didn't even have much to drink. Maybe it was the thought of my new "sole" mate. Next time, I'm going to get rat-arsed, then at least I'll have a reason to feel this rough. The whole pleasure/pain thing is becoming just pain. I'm late, too, so I don't have time to do my make-up. Obviously, Mick's going to have something to say about that.

'Ooh, Bob, you look like a bulldog licking piss off a thistle.'

'How original,' I say.

'Seriously, though, rough.'

'You're no George Clooney yourself.' I throw him the most disdainful look I can manage.

'That was a dirty one. Hacky black, as my old nan used to say. If looks could kill, I'd be decomposing as we speak.'

'Smells like you are,' I say.

'Now, now, Bob. You know you love me, really.'

'Yeah, like I love toothache.'

'Don't say you wouldn't,' Mick says, clearly alluding to the fact that he thinks I'd sleep with him.

'I really wouldn't.'

'You *so* would.'

'I *so* would not.'

'Who is this date for the dinner dance?'

'Never mind, you'll find out soon enough.'

'If he exists.'

'Oh, yeah, cos I'm such a munter, I have to go around inventing boyfriends.' I try not to choke while saying that. 'I'm meeting him tonight, actually. In Café Rouge.' Why? Why did I say that?

'Café Rouge, eh? Jonathon,' he shouts to the Foetus. 'You fancy French tonight?'

'French what?' Johnathon asks. 'If it's kiss, I'm good, thanks.'

'French food. Café Rouge.'

'Yeah, sounds like a plan.'

'What did you go and do that for?' I ask.

'Thought your boyfriend could do with a little moral support.'

'And how are you going to support his morals when you have none of your own?'

'So bitter. You really need to work on your people skills.'

'Get lost.'

'People skills, Roberta.' I turn away before I jump on him and gouge out his eyes. At least he's dropped "Bob".

'See you tonight,' he says sweetly, blowing me a kiss. I mime catching it, throwing it to the floor and stamping on it.

#datingdisaster

I took a selfie alone in the restaurant waiting for the ex-boyfriend to show. I uploaded it to Twitter, Facebook and Instagram and got no likes.

Of course, the evening was a disaster. That goes without saying. Harry arrived late, so I sat on my own for half an hour while Mick and co whispered and laughed. I imagined them saying, 'See, I told you she'd made him up.'

When he did arrive, he wasn't bad looking, but his craic was as boring as watching wallpaper dry. I had to sit through a chronology of his movements since the day we split up thirty years ago. He hadn't led an interesting life. The highlight was a trip to Malaga – 'You might have seen it in the papers' – where he'd been arrested for trying to hump a dolphin. Of course, he was innocent. I bet.

I was going to make my excuses and leave – 'the house is on fire', 'the cactus needs water' – but Mick and co came over. 'So, you're Roberta's boyfriend,' Mick said. 'How lovely to meet you.'

'I am?' Harry said, looking at me quizzically. I smiled or grimaced; it's probably hard to tell the difference with me. 'I am,' he said with confidence, holding out his hand to shake Mick's.

'I wouldn't shake that,' I said. 'You don't know where it's been.'

'Ha-ha, *you* do, though, Bob. You can vouch for me,' Mick said. I wanted to punch a hole where his nose was. 'I imagine you'll be taking Bob to the company ball?' he asked Harry.

'Oh, er…well,' Harry stuttered. I did that smile/grimace again. Embarrassment strangled me. 'Yes, yes, of course.'

Aw, bloody hell. How am I going to get out of this?

Chapter 12

#wetwetwet

I'm reading Mother's letters. Even they will be less tragic than my life right now.

Letter number eight:
6th January, 1941
Dear Michael,
Today, I am celebrating. Joy of all joys. You are coming on Monday. I can't wait to see you there at the station. We will have the best fun here together in the countryside. I will teach you how to ride the bull. He's called Angus, and he'll throw you off if you're not too careful. The Mister says I'm the best at riding him. The Missus says it's because I can cling like a leech. I'm a bloodsucker, she says. I wouldn't suck her blood, it'll taste bitter.
Yours,
Alice

Letter number nine:
10th January, 1941
Dear Michael,
The Missus tells me you've taken a turn for the worse, and that Mother says you'll have to stay another week or so. It was such a disappointment to me when they told me you wouldn't be on the train after all. I ran down to the station and waited just in case and then suffered a thick ear from the Missus on my return. She said the butter was spoiled, and it was all my fault.
Yours,
Alice

Dear Alice,
The bombing is intensifying. Every night, the siren sounds, and we have to go to the shelter. Some families have had enough. The Thompsons and the Fosters have packed up their belongings, and they're moving out of their flats. The two misters have hired a van. They've piled everything in: bedding, blankets, clothes, saucepans, kettles, chairs, the kids and the missus. The babby sits in the middle, clutching a teddy bear with one eye. They've even taken the canary in a cage. Mrs Linton says it reminds her of the song, and she starts to sing it in the shelter. It's all about following her old man in a van. Then, they're singing about Tipperary. Then, we're packing up our troubles in our old kit bag and smiling. They're cheerful songs, though, and it lightens the mood as we're sitting in the dank shelter waiting for the bombing to subside.

Mr Cant starts a song about there always being an England. I'm not so sure. The noise tonight suggests it'll be flattened by the time we emerge bleary eyed into the daylight. I imagine you running through fields and meadows, surrounded by hedgerows and blossoms. Collecting caterpillars and frolicking in woods, picking bluebells and making daisy chains. I'm both sad and happy you're not here.
Your loving brother,
Michael

Letter number ten:
15th January, 1941
Dear Michael,
I found out that one of the kids with no shoes is called Bertie. His family is so poor that none of the children have shoes, and the reason his head is shaved is because his hair was crawling with lice. Nits, they call them around here. There's a nurse comes to school to check our heads. Nitty Nora the Head Explorer we call her. The reason he wears his jumper back to front is so that no one can see that he has no vest or shirt on.

The wool itches him terribly, and his torso is covered in sores. The other kids mock him and make a big song and dance if they have to sit near him. Me, I'd rather sit with him than any of them. He says he's going to be somebody one day, and I believe him.
Yours,
Alice

Letter number eleven:
5th February, 1941
Dear Michael,
Bertie is a crack shot. We go rabbiting together, and he sells the catch to the Missus, so his family can eat eggs and bread and milk. We go fishing in the river. It belongs to the lord (not the one we pray to, but a posh fella with a great big house), but as long as we don't get caught, he won't mind.

Bertie is the cleverest in the class, even though all the masters pick on him because he's poor. He says he is going to be a solicitor when he leaves school. He says he's going to move away to London and make something of himself. I've said he can come and live with us. Mother and Father will like him, and you will too. Can't wait for the two of you to meet.
Yours,
Alice

Dear Alice,
I learned a new word last night: Looters. Dad says they're the lowest of the low. They raid homes and shops during the air raid and steal things. One was caught tonight wearing an ARP Warden's armband and helmet. The crowd wanted to lynch him, but Mr Jones managed to persuade them to turn him over to the coppers. They led him off in a Black Maria, but next time I saw him, he was black and blue. They say he fell down the stairs at the station. Dad says there are no stairs at the station.

Tonight, the air rumbles and trembles like a giant thunderstorm brewing. It crackles and fizzes like fireworks. Flashes cast crimson reflections on the buildings in the square. The East End is a sea of blood. All along the road, there's brick dust and rubble. People's homes are split down the middle, their bedrooms exposed to public view: wardrobes reduced to splinters, chamber pots and crockery smashed to smithereens. Black smoke shrouds the whole of the common, and all the clocks have stopped. It feels like the end of the world.

Till we meet again, dear sister.

Your loving brother,
Michael

Letter number twelve:
03/04/1941 Telegram from London: Bad news stop fatal attack on Lime Street stop no survivors stop

Letter number thirteen:
4th April, 1941
Dear Michael,
I can't stop imagining you all sitting round the table in the kitchen. Mother cuts off a chunk of bread and spreads it with molten dripping. Father laughs at you eating at last. Mother smiles, but there's sadness behind the smile as she realises you will have to join me in the countryside, now that you're well enough. She knows it would be selfish to keep you there where you're at risk of being bombed.

I see the chink in the blackout curtains. I see the pilot in the air noticing the light. I see his expression change as he realises his target. I see the bomb drop, and the house disintegrate. The walls crumble in on themselves, and I see your hand, blue and limp, reaching out from the rubble. I see Mother's eyes, glassy and lifeless, Father's inert limbs. I wake crying and sweating. The Missus comes running, threatening me with the belt if

I make any more of my noise. I'll scream silently every night hereafter and call your name into the darkness.
Yours,
Alice

Letter number fourteen:
10th April, 1941
Dear Michael,
I don't know how it happened. I only know what the telegram told me. I imagine you crouching under the stairs or in a cold, damp shelter while aerial pounding falls all around you with deafening cracks, bangs and flashes of light. Mrs Timms's baby screaming beside you as she tries in vain to quieten it with a bottle. Mother and Father holding hands, a fortress of love against the Nazis. The realisation that you are about to die. The fear. The dust. The terror. The next one has your name on it. You know. You accept. You wait.

They tell us the war will soon be over. My war will never be over now.
Yours,
Alice

***

Poor Mother. I can't imagine the pain she must have gone through. Stuck in a place she hated, where she was neglected and abused, then receiving the news her whole family was dead. Tears pour down my face. I wish I'd known. If only she'd told us what she suffered, I'd have understood her better.

Shoni rings to say let bygones be bygones and do I want to meet halfway for a day's shopping? I'd rather pluck my pubic hair with a plumbing tool, but after reading Mother's letters, it hit me how important it is to spend time with your family. I've also promised myself I'll try to be nice, so I tell her I'd love to.

The car's had another hot flush and collapsed, so I've had to take the train. When I get there, I'm sweating like a blind lesbian at a whelk stall.

'You been swimming?' Shoni asks.

'No.'

'Oh, right. It's just that you're wet.'

'So are you, but that's nothing new.'

'Mother, be nice.'

'You started it.'

'I didn't. I just thought…oh, never mind. Let's just get to the shops, shall we? Kevin will take your bag.'

'That's what I'm worried about.'

'Come again?'

'Nothing.' My mouth is firmly closed. No accusations about the drug-dealing degenerate shall pass my lips.

'I thought we could go in Mystique to look at the mother of the bride outfits.'

'Ok.' Best to say as little as possible then I can't be blamed for causing World War Three.

It should be called Mistake, because the outfits there are big bloopers. If I wanted to look like a stuffed manatee, then perhaps they'd suffice. Sea monster, however, is not my look of choice for my firstborn's first wedding (I'm under no illusion that it will be her last).

I bite my tongue – really. I try on a couple of dresses that look like a blancmange and an STI respectively. I merely say I don't think they suit my skin tone. I'm on my best behaviour, I promise. I don't mention custard substitutes or syphilis. And I could. I don't say I'd rather eat my own ovaries than wear those creations. I'm distinctly polite, and still, my daughter berates me like an angry head teacher.

'Why do you have to be so sarcastic? Why do you always make a fuss? Why can't you just be happy for me?'

'Why do you have to ask rhetorical questions?'

'I just wish I had a loving mother. A mother who cares, who wants to do things with me and for me. It's not enough, Mother, to feed and clothe us, to make sure we're educated, to brush our teeth and our hair. Our souls need nourishment.'

'Really? I didn't look after your feet?'

'Why can't you be serious for one minute?'

'I didn't know we were raking over old coals. I thought, stupidly, we were here to try on dresses.'

'All I've ever wanted was a mother who cared.' *Join the club.*

'That's not entirely true. You wanted a Pippa doll, a pink sequined jewellery box and a Chihuahua.'

'I wanted a mother who was prepared to be there for her child.'

'Children.' One gets the feeling my eldest won't be happy until I've nailed myself to a cross in her honour. 'Best be getting back,' I say.

'Yes, that's right, as soon as the conversation turns to anything serious, let's just brush it under the carpet.'

Actually, if the truth be known, it isn't just the conversation that has me heading out but also my need to pee. Lately, when I've got to go, I've really got to go. I don't want a repeat of the gym fiasco. 'I'll just nip to the loo.'

'That's right, bury your head in the sand.' I'm not burying anything. Except perhaps my womanhood in the ruddy great tomb of the menopause.

'I'll come back,' I say. 'Get me the green one again in a size twelve.'

'A twelve?' Shoni says, her voice shrieking incredulously.

'Yes, daughter dear, a twelve.'

'You do know they're snug sizes?'

'Ok, I'll try the fourteen too.'

'She'll have the sixteen,' Shoni says as I leave the store. I'm tempted to carry on walking and not go back, but I must have somehow acquired a modicum of maternal instinct. I'm determined the sixteen will be too big if I have to chop off a limb and have liposuction on the way back from the loo.

It turns out the sixteen is too tight. Shoni stands there, oozing smugness, while I try to squeeze my bum cheeks through the gap. It won't go up, so I try to pull it down. The ripping sound resonates round the whole shop, and the assistant comes running – to haul back the curtains and show my bum cheeks to the world. There's a piece of sleeve wrapped round my face that looks like a lion's mane. You'd think I'd taken a pee in the corner of the cubicle, the way she's going on. She threatens me with the police if I don't pay for the damaged goods. So, now, I have half a mother of the bride outfit and badly bruised pride.

Tammy calls to say she got off with the Foetus last night, and they ended up at her flat. She was hammered, so she couldn't remember whether they'd done it or not, but she was sure they must have as she has a bout of cystitis brewing.

For the rest of the day, I shall be mainly drinking wine, eating chocolate and feeling sorry for myself.

Chapter 13

#breakdown

No one tells you about the menopausal sickness. You hear about the hot flushes and the night sweats, the moustache and the loss of sex drive, but no one talks about the nausea and sickness. I wake up this morning feeling like I'm going to throw up every time I move. I shove a couple of ginger biscuits down my neck and jump in the old jalopy. She coughs and splutters into life and then purrs like a kitten. The purring, however, ceases at the traffic lights where she cuts out and refuses to move. I try coaxing, stroking, whispering, and when that doesn't work, I get out and kick her.

A policeman (muscular, manly, dishy) wanders up to me and asks what the problem is and can he help.

'She's broken down,' I say.

'Let's have a look,' he says, jumping behind the steering wheel and turning the key. I surreptitiously take a selfie of him and me. 'Oh, aye, ah see what the problem is.'

'You do?'

'Aye.'

'And do you know how to fix it?'

'Aye.'

'That's great.'

'Come here,' he says. I do as he bids, wondering if this is just a ploy. Maybe he likes older women. 'See that little line there?'

'Yes.'

'And see that gauge there?'

'Yes.'

'It sez empty.' He jumps out of the car and points to the petrol cap. 'See this 'ere?'

'Yes.'

'You put petrol in 'ere, and the car will gan.'

'Thank you.' Sarcastic Geordie twat.

It costs me £180 to have her towed to the nearest garage so I can fill up. I'm late for work again, and Oldham gives me a first written warning while I retch over the waste-paper bin. Unfeeling, insensitive pig.

I post the selfie of me and the local Bobby. There are no likes on Facebook yet. Maybe his helmet's not big enough.

#whocares?

People have been breathing all day. It makes me want to kill them. A swift knife to the ribs and an upward tear resulting in tortured screams and gurgling, frothy, bloody spit. Anything's got to be better than this constant breathing. The pen tapping is also criminal. If the Foetus taps his pen on the desk one more time, I'm going to have him aborted.

The sneezing is infuriating too. That prat from payroll has hay fever. Sabina Somethingorother. I'm so sick of her snot-ridden, sniffling, sneezy conversations. She's telling me about her husband's mother's cat's cancer, and I think, who cares? No one gives a tiny rat's testicle. The thing is, I don't just think it, I say it aloud. So now, she's put in a grievance, and Oldham wants to speak with me tomorrow. Some people need to grow a pair.

Of course, Mick thinks it's hilarious. 'I told you, you needed to brush up on your people skills,' he says. 'I bet they send you on a course.' Jesus, that's all I need, to spend the day with a bunch of ignorant bigots. At least I'm consistent. I hate everyone.

I receive another weird email. The subject line says: "You know how subtle are the links that bind two souls which are so closely allied". Haven't a clue what it means or who sent it, but I'm not even going to try to open it in case it is a virus.

I've been on a few other dates, most of them too embarrassing to document. There was Psycho, Sicko and Face-licker. Litigator was probably the worst of a bad bunch. I think his given name was Carl or Craig. He picked me up in his Subaru with gold (I kid you not) dashboard and fur-lined seats. He had something green stuck between his two front teeth. I tried to gesture, but he was too thick-skinned (or just plain thick) to realise, so I had to tell him. He checked in the huge mirror tucked behind his sun visor and offered, 'Guac,' as an explanation before screeching away and doing seventy in second gear.

When we got to the Odeon, he paid for the ticket (one point in his favour. Tight Wad had just had to "nip to the loo" and left me to pay for us both). He bought popcorn and asked me if I'd like a hotdog. I declined, remembering Tammy's dictum that they're made from pigs' lips and bums.

I didn't want to see anything erotic, in case he got the wrong idea. I didn't want a repeat of Shoe Boy. We settled on *It*, the remake of the Stephen King classic. I'm not scared easily, and clowns don't freak me out the way they do Tammy. He might have hoped I'd cuddle up to him, but he was mistaken.

I'm not that keen on popcorn, as it happens. It's a bit like chewing polystyrene and the kernels get stuck in my teeth. After a few irate looks from him for rattling the box, I tried to just suck the caramel to lessen the noise.

When he complained about me texting during the film, I decided to leave. I nipped to the loo, texted Tammy and waited outside for her to show up.

We'd just arrived at mine, cracked open a smooth Rioja and were sipping while swapping stories about sad bastards, when I got a text from the Litigator telling me I owed him, '£10 for the cinema ticket and £4.99 for the popcorn.'

I showed Tammy the message, and she burst out laughing, spluttering red wine onto my new top. 'Oh my God, you can certainly pick them.'

'I blame you,' I said.

'Me?' she said. 'I merely led you to the water. I did not drop poison in it.'

Because I ignored the text, he sent me a barrage of abusive messages calling me everything from a freeloader to a dirty toe-sucking whore. I blocked his number, of course, but it didn't end there. A letter from the County Court duly informed me the Litigator was taking me to court for the price of a cinema ticket, popcorn and for the emotional damage caused to his person as a result of my inappropriate, inconsiderate and appalling behaviour. My behaviour (texting during the film and ruining it for other people as well as violating the cinema's policy) apparently was a threat to civilised society. You could not make this shit up.

The next date, the Mansplainer, wasn't nearly as much trouble as the Litigator but was as irritating as thrush on a dirty weekend. We arranged to meet at my local. He explained how to get there using a map and compass.

'I have GPS,' I said, 'if I get lost in the next hundred yards.' He then mansplained the history of said local pub, even though I told him I was responsible in part for creating the historical pamphlet which explains that it was a place where coachmen stopped on their way from London to Edinburgh. He mansplained Chateaubriand is a tenderloin cut of beef. He mansplained what the sauce should contain. I swear, if I hadn't thrown him a filthy look, he'd have mansplained to the nursing mother at a nearby table how to breastfeed her child. By this point, I was ready to leave the perfect steak and head home. I texted Tammy, and she rang me. He mansplained dinner etiquette and mobile phones.

'Sorry, I've got to go,' I said. 'Speak soon.' I immediately blocked him on Tinder, Facebook and Instagram. How had I not noticed his mansplaining in his emails?

'He is quite hot,' Tammy said. 'Maybe you were swayed by the topless torso pics.' I immediately deleted all males with topless torso profile pics.

#moodswings

My doctor prescribes me a course of antidepressants. Me. Depressed? I don't feel depressed. Those "woe is me" types exasperate me. The "I must have been terrible in a former life" types who sit and bewail every misfortune to become them. Needless to say, I don't go to the chemists. Fluoxetine, indeed. He said they would improve my mood.

There's nothing wrong with my fucking mood, I wanted to say.

I'm changing doctors.

#blackdeath

I'm called into the office and spoken to about my treatment of the prat from payroll. I say in my defence she was sneezing and spreading germs all over the office. Oldham says that's not a defence, and if she decides to pursue it, I could be dismissed for gross misconduct. I'm sure spreading the bubonic plague is gross misconduct, but she's not getting into trouble. Bet he's sleeping with her. Eeew, I do not want that mental picture. He says I have to apologise. 'Over my dead body,' I say. He says he'll give me the weekend to think about what it would be like to be out of work in this climate and approaching fifty. Cheeky sod. How does he know I'm nearly fifty? I look nothing like my age. I tell him he's lucky I haven't been headhunted by now.

'Get real, Gallbreath. It's a wonder you haven't been given the chop.'

#grammargripes

I get a text from Drew asking to lend a tenner. 'Who you gonna lend it to?' I text.

He rings me and says, 'For God's sake, Mother, I'm on the bones of my arse, and you're correcting my grammar.'

'Get a job, son,' I say.

'I've tried.'

'You should be still trying. And don't give up until you get one.'

'Huh.'

'Well, it's been lovely conversing with you on this fine Saturday, but I must go. I have things to do.'

He cuts me off before I finish speaking.

'Ten pounds transferred to your account,' I text. I wait for the *thank you,* but it doesn't arrive. Bloody typical.

Letter number fifteen:
10th May, 1941
Dear Michael,
How could you leave me? I am half of a whole. A mere fraction of the person I was. Incomplete forever. An orphan. A lonely orphan. Twinless. Hopeless. I blame Mother and Father, but mainly Mother. She wanted you close because you were ill. Why couldn't she just have put you on the train with me? I'd have looked after you. Why? Why you? Why them? Why me? Why?

I am jealous. Jealous that you are dead and that I am still here. People might think I am ungrateful. I am jealous of Mother and Father that they got to die with you. I am jealous of you that you got to die with Mother and Father. I am angry that I am left here alone. And then I am consumed by guilt. Guilt about my anger. Guilt about my jealousy. Guilt I have survived. And I miss you. More than when you were in London and there was the promise of your arrival. More than when I first left, and I expected to see you again soon. I miss you with the cold, stark reality that I will never see you again. The "if onlys" will drive me crazy in the forthcoming days, weeks and months.

Years will have to pass before I can think of you without tears. And even then, a black hole will open and swallow me at times. 'Life goes on,' people will say, and I will want to slap them. Why couldn't the war end earlier? Why did it have to take you and Mother and Father? Why leave me?
Yours,
Alice

Letter number sixteen:
1st January, 1949
Dear Michael,
I know you'll never read this, but who else can I write to? Who else will listen? I hear the Missus and Mister arguing about me. He's telling her I need to be watched.

'Have you seen her?' he says. 'Boys stare when we go to town. I'm telling you there'll be trouble.'

'Never mind,' she says. 'I've got it sorted.' I have no idea what they mean, but it doesn't sound good.
Yours,
Alice

Letter number seventeen:
5th January, 1951
Dear Bertie,
Thank you for your kind invitation to walk out with you. The Mister and Missus are very strict, and I am sure if I were to ask their permission, they would not grant it, so I must say no, but it was a kind offer and one I am grateful for.
Yours sincerely,
Alice

Letter number eighteen:
8th March, 1951
Dear Bertie,
I can see why you might be disappointed in my decision not to ask them, but I fear that they might keep me under lock and key to ensure that I do not sneak out to meet you. You may think I am being histrionic, but you do not know them. I can assure you they will not grant me permission to go out with you.
Yours sincerely,
Alice

Letter number nineteen:
10th May, 1951
Dear Bertie,
While I can understand why you felt the need to visit the Mister and Missus to ask their permission to take me out, I fear that it has made matters worse for me. My stepsisters mock me, and my guardians berate me. Would you do me the kindness of never repeating the experiment?
Respectfully yours,
Alice

Letter number twenty
20th October, 1951

Dear Bertie,
I will meet you by the entrance to the churchyard at midnight. I will sneak out when they are all fast asleep. The sisters sleep soundly and snore like dragons. The Mister and Missus sleep less soundly, but are in another room so I should be able to make my escape.
Yours,
Alice

Letter number twenty-one
10th November, 1951
Dear Bertie,
"We are such stuff as dreams are made on." I had the most amazing night. Thank you for your chivalry. Yes, I would like to do it again soon.
Yours,
Alice

Letter number twenty-two
21st March, 1952
Dear Bertie,
I had an amazing time. You are such a gentleman. In every way. My parents would have approved of you. No, I do not think it is premature of you to declare your love for me. If I was not a shy girl and decent, I would most certainly do the same and declare my love for you.
Yours,
Alice

Letter number twenty-three
15th June, 1952
My Darling Bertie,
You are the first thing I think about when I wake each morning and the last thing I think about before I am "rounded with sleep".
Yours forever,
Alice

Letter number twenty-four
11th July, 1952
Dearest Darling Bertie,
We have been discovered. One of the sisters saw me leaving the house and followed me. She threatens to tell the Mister and Missus, unless I tell you I can never see you again. I have promised her that I will. My promises to her are like dust. We must be more careful in future. I know I am of an age where I could do as I wish, but I have nowhere to go, no money and the Mister threatens to kill any man I step out with. This is a very real threat. I worry for you.
All my love forever,
Alice

Letter number twenty-five
5th August, 1952
My Dearest Darling Bertie,
Thank you, thank you, a million times thank you. The answer to your question is yes.

Get thee to church on Thursday where I shall be proud to make thee "a joyful bride". Once we are married, there is nothing they can do about it. It will be legal and above board. I'm sure they will come around then and maybe find it in their hearts to be happy for me. Or at least to let me go.
Yours forever,
Alice

Letter number twenty-six
21st August, 1952
My Dearest Darling Bertie,
I cannot tell you how sorry I am. Wicked sisters found out about our plan to marry and locked me in the coal cellar. Had the circumstances been different, you would have laughed to

see me covered head to toe in black dust looking every inch a coal man. "Screw your courage to the sticking place, and we will not fail", next time.
All my love forever,
Alice

Letter number twenty-seven
12th November, 1952
My Dearest Darling Bertie,
This is probably the hardest thing I have ever had to write. Much as I'd like to, and you know this to be true, I cannot be with you. They are forcing me to marry against my will. They have threatened that if I run away, they will hunt me down, and they will kill you. "Hang, beg, starve, die in the streets" – I cannot risk you being hurt and must make this sacrifice in your honour. I think money has exchanged hands. I know him to be a cruel and heartless man, and I don't expect to have a happy marriage or a fulfilling life, but the moments spent with you will last me forever. I will remember your smile, your face, your touch until the end of time. Much love always. Try to bear the loss as I must.
Your only love,
Alice

Letter number twenty-eight
June 1953
My Dearest Darling Bertie,
We must be secretive if we are to continue to see each other. I have a husband in name only. He will never be my love. We will be unable to meet very often, but I shall be as pleased to see you once a year, if that is all I am to be allowed.
All my love forever,
Alice

Letter number twenty-nine
17th June, 1967
My Dearest Darling Bertie,
I understand that you can no longer stomach our arrangement. I understand how difficult it must be for you to go home alone and to imagine me here with him. But know that every minute I spend with him, I am wishing I was with you.

I don't quite know how to tell you this, but I'm having your baby. It makes no difference to our situation, but I know the child is yours. This child is made from love, not from his tired, messy and brutal fumblings in the dark. I will love her (for I'm sure it is a girl) enough for both of us.
Yours forever,
Alice

I'm in shock. I didn't know that Mother was a Shakespeare fan. Not once did I see her pick up a book. How romantic she once was. Was my father not my father? Who was this Bertie? I can't read on. I replace the letters in their envelope and close the drawer.

Chapter 14

#waterbabe #giantcondom

The doctor has recommended swimming as a way to release tension and exercise without aggravating joint pain. I decide to use the pool at Lloyds, rather than my local swimming pool to prevent being ducked by delinquent teens or splashed by the "turtle-time" brigade. I'm trying to keep my mind off Mother's revelation. I remember the conversation in the hospital before she died. 'It wasn't your dad's watch. Well, it was. But not the man you thought was your dad.' My mind is reeling. Who was my father? Where do I really come from?

The only swimming hat left to purchase is luminous green, so I look like a giant condom. I pray I don't see anyone I know.

#newbossblow

Today is the worst day ever. Not only have I been made to apologise to the prat from payroll, but an announcement has been made that our lines of reporting are to change as from today. Our new line manager is to be...I can't even type it without being a little bit sick in my mouth...Mick the Dick.

He's sitting there in his new suit, sporting a goatee and smirking.

'Good news, eh, Bob?'

'The best,' I say sarcastically. 'Now, show me how to get up on the roof terrace.' His eyebrows meet in the middle. 'So, I can jump off,' I enlighten him.

'Don't be like that,' he says, feigning a hurt look. 'We make a great team.'

'So did Bonnie and Clyde.'

'Now, now, Bob.'

'Will you stop calling me that?'

'Well, it's better than your nickname.'

'What nickname? I don't have a nickname.'

'Oh, yes, you do.'

'I don't.'

'You do. No one knows their own nickname. I bet you have one for me. Probably something unoriginal…'

'No, I wouldn't be so childish.'

'Like Mick the Prick.'

'So, what's mine?' I ask.

'It's not for me to say. It might upset you.'

'As if I give a stuff what you lot think of me.'

'Let's just leave it, shall we. Can you have the Booker report on my desk by close of play today?' I hate that phrase, "close of play". Tosser.

'Bellissmo,' I say, then retire to the ladies' to bang my head off the walls.

#resigned

I take a selfie on the bus with the barking mad.

I take it back. Monday was not the worst day ever. Today is the worst day ever! The heightened sense of smell is back, and I have to sit next to dog-breath woman on the bus. A whippet chews the bow on my new shoes, and his drunken owner says he's going to sue me if his dog is sick.

'Never mind the bloody dog. Those shoes cost four hundred quid.' (That's a lie. They cost me sixty quid on eBay, *excellent condition, worn once*.) Of course, the marauding hordes are only concerned about the dog and not my Jimmy Choos, so I have to walk in to work bowless.

'Personal grooming,' Mick says as I sweep in, windblown and worrisome.

'I had an altercation with an animal,' I say, then mutter, 'not for the first time.'

'Let's not have excuses,' he says.

'Let's not talk to us as though we're three years old,' I say.

'My office please, Roberta.' Ooh, things are looking up. My full name. 'Take a seat.'

'I'd rather stand.'

'As you wish.'

'It has come to my attention, Ms Gallbreath…'

'Are you kidding me? Ms Gallbreath?'

'Let's just keep this as professional as possible under the circumstances. It has come to my attention that you have been upsetting a number of our employees with your comments and criticisms.'

'What the…'

'Furthermore, your use of pejoratives…'

'Are you fucking kidding me?'

'Roberta, please. You're not making this easy.'

'Oh sorry, beg your pardon, *I'm* making things difficult for *you*. That's rich, that is.'

'I have no idea what you mean.'

'I mean that since you set foot in this company, you have done nothing but make my life a misery.'

He looks shocked. 'I'm sorry you feel that way.' He looks genuinely sorry. Bloody good actor. 'Perhaps we should do this another time.'

'Perhaps we should. Do what? Are you sacking me? Are you? Tell you what, you can't sack me, cos I quit.' There's that shocked expression again. Give this lad a BAFTA. I stand up, swipe the papers from his desk onto the floor, storm out and try to slam the door, but my foot is caught in it, and I only succeed in bruising my shin.

I'm now at home crying into a cheeky Vimto and wondering how I'm going to get another job at my age. Me and my bloody big mouth.

#popidle

I take a selfie in the unemployment office with Newcastle's answer to Stevie Wonder.

I sign on the dole for the first time in thirty years. It's a humiliating experience, and they don't call it dole anymore. The woman's expression suggests she has a dead kipper under her nose.

'So, you left of your own accord?'

'Yes.'

'They didn't sack you?'

'No, they were about to, but I got in first. I didn't want that on my record.'

'You won't be entitled to benefits.'

'Why?'

'Because you had a job, and you left of your own accord.'

'But they were going to sack me anyway.'

'It doesn't matter, they didn't. Next.' She looks beyond me to the man with the Labrador standing behind me. 'No dogs allowed.'

'It's a guide dog,' he says.

'No dogs,' she says. 'Can't you read?'

'He can't see, you daft cow, so how's he supposed to read the sign?'

'You'll have to take him outside.'

'But I need to sign on.'

'I'll hold him for you,' I say.

'I can't come down the stairs without him.'

'He can't come down the stairs without him,' I say.

'He isn't blind. He's lying,' she says. 'If you don't leave, I'll call security.'

'Don't move,' I say to the man. 'She can't do a thing.'

So, that's how I end up in a police cell next door to a drunken butcher and a pretend blind man. It seems he won't leave his dog tied up outside, in case it gets stolen, so he pretends to be visually impaired. You couldn't make this stuff up.

#probonio

Police Cellfie! (See what I did there?)

Luckily, I still have the number of Shoni's friend's dad, and he arrives with his briefcase and a stern expression minutes after I'm allowed to make my phone call. He tells the police to charge me or release me, otherwise he'll be claiming wrongful arrest and harassment. Not only that, but he'll be contacting his cousin who works for the *Daily Mirror* and giving him a story of inhuman DSS workers and police brutality.

When I get home, there's a message on the answerphone from Mick. 'Roberta, would you please call me. You have my number.' Is this a dig? Or does he just want me to collect my things from the office. There's no way I'm showing my face in there. They can keep my "Office Bitch" mug and the photos of my kids.

I receive another weird email from the same address with the subject line: "So we grew together like to a double cherry, seeming parted".

WTF?

#situationvacant

My hunt for a new job started today. It was a sobering business. For all the experience I have, on paper, I'm not that attractive. Having worked for the same company for the majority of my adult life and working my way up from being a glorified tea girl, I have plenty of skills and knowledge but not so many formal qualifications. I'm looking in the situations vacant section at the positions I'm qualified for. I'm almost ready to go cap in hand to Mick and beg his forgiveness. I say almost. Hell doesn't have snowmen just yet.

Letter number thirty
October 1967
My Dearest Bertie,
The doctor thinks I am having twins. He says I am far too big, and he can feel two heads. At first, I was afraid I was giving birth to a monster, but now, I am sure that he is right, and I am to have two babies. I hope it will be a boy and a girl. The boy will look like you and the girl like me. I'm reminded of my own dear twin. The brother I lost. He would have loved you so much, as you would have loved him. How sad I am that the two of you never got to meet. How sad I am that he will never share in the pleasure of our twins.

You are, and always will be, in my thoughts daily. My love for you will never be diminished, even though he tries to beat it from me. The floggings only serve to make it stronger. He complains about everything. The way I look, the way I eat, the way I speak. Nothing is good enough for him. He accuses me of having a mouth full of marbles and of thinking I'm better than everyone up here. He beats me if he hears a trace of my "pretentious southern drawl". I've all but lost my accent, and I've lost myself.
Yours forever,
Alice

Letter number thirty-one
April 1968
Dearest Bertie,
The twins are born, and they are the most beautiful children in the whole world. Michaela is the most delicate and sweet little girl you ever did see. Robert (he forced me to name him for him) is imperfect but perfect to me. He has something called a cleft palate and harelip. It will require surgery, but I'm sure he will recover and be fine. I have never felt so happy, and I never thought I could be happy without you. The children are a piece of you that I'll carry with me every day. You would be a perfect father to them, and when they are old enough, I will tell them all about you, and I will tell them about their hero uncle who bravely saved a family during the war, but then lost his own life before he could escape to the country.
Yours forever,
Alice

Letter number thirty-two
May 1968
Dear Bertie,
My heart is broken. This is the darkest day of my life to date. Darker than the day I lost my brother and my parents in the London air raid, darker than the day I was forced to marry the beast or than the day I lost you. Robert has taken against our baby boy. He calls him ugly and a monster. He says he won't have him in the house. He says I must change their names. The girl must be called Roberta, for him, and the boy must be "got rid of". I have begged and pleaded. I was sure he would change his mind but to no avail. He says he will find someone to take him. If you get this in time, I want you to come for him. Look after him for me. You must come quickly before he has chance to find someone to take him.
Yours,
Alice

I unfold a sheet of brown paper and realise on it is a family tree. I work out from the names that it's my mother's family. Under my father's name is Felicity, but our mother's name isn't there. Under our mother's name is my name and the name Michael, but my father's name isn't there. The name Bertram Stonehouse is next to Mother's and above mine.

I have a twin brother!

Letter number thirty-three
Dear Mr Gallbreath,
My husband and I are free to speak with you about the adoption this coming Saturday. If you could confirm a time and meeting place that would be convenient to you, we will certainly be there.
Yours sincerely,
Mrs Oliver Rowbotham

Letter number thirty-four
July 1968
Bertie,
You are too late. My heart is broken. It cannot be fixed this time. I am trying hard to forgive you for this. You may not have received my letter. They came and took Michael from me. Plucked him from my arms as I screamed. Robert called me hysterical and hit me with a horsewhip when they had gone. He cannot hurt me any more than the pain of losing my son. Nothing can hurt more than this. Nothing. Roberta cried all night. It's as though she realises she has lost her brother. I can sympathise with her, but it is nothing compared to the pain of losing a son. I have decided I will love no one else. Love only ever ends in pain. This will be my final communication to you. I wish you more happiness than I will ever experience, though that is not necessarily much.
Alice

I used to read novels where characters said they were reeling. I had no idea what this meant until now. I read all the letters again. I'm shaking. I sit. My mouth's open. I only realise this when my tongue goes dry and feels cold. Who knows how long I sit here like this. Mother always used to say that everything looks better in the morning, so I'm going to bed in the hope that this is true.

#doesntlookbetter

Still reeling. Staying in bed.

Letter number thirty-five
15th June, 1972
Bertie,
It's a physical pain I live with every day. A dark tunnel I'm in with no light at the end. I feel it closing in on me. My arms ache for Michael. Roberta grows steadily. I feed her, I clean her, I clothe her, but I cannot love her. I cannot love. I will not love again. Love is pain. He has brought the child of an affair to live with us. I know not what happened to the mother. I know better than to ask questions. She is called Felicity, and I feel ashamed to say I hate the child.
Alice

#sickasachip

I feel sick. I drink some ginger tea, which is supposed to settle your stomach, but I throw it back up. I only just manage to make it to the bathroom in time. My head hurts, and my chest is tight. I'm going back to bed.

I once read on one of those psychobabble websites that you can only hold one thought in your head at a time and that you're responsible for what that thought is. I've decided this is not true. My head abounds with a menagerie of thoughts, and I can't get it to be still. Where do I start? What do I do? Felicity isn't really my sister. Not my full sister. Not my biological sister at all. And I have a twin. A twin brother. What happened to him?

Letter number 36
June 1975
Bertie,
I am still in the tunnel. He is a brute. His dinner must be on the table and the correct temperature for him coming through the door. His pipe must be prepared, and his slippers warmed by the fire. He must have his newspaper. Everything must be perfect for him. Everything is terrible for me. How can I bear forty years of this? I know I said I would communicate no more, but who else do I have to tell?

He has taken to drinking on Friday afternoons when he receives his pay packet. He rolls home, bounces off the door frame and staggers into the kitchen. He throws looks of hatred in my direction. I'm not quite sure what I have done to attract his hatred. I do as I am bid, all day, every day. Perhaps it is because he knows that I do not love him. I do not love anyone or anything. Myself included.

It usually begins by my being pinned to a wall or door by the throat and ends with me picking myself up off the floor and wiping blood from the tiles. God help me if Roberta cries and wakes him as he snoozes by the fire.

I dread going to bed. I try my hardest not to wake him. I make myself as light as air as I perch on the edge of the bed and try not to roll in his direction. If I wake him, I will have to endure the monstrous act. This, more than anything else, kills my spirit and drowns my hopes.

His daughter is a mean-spirited little thing. She pinches Roberta whenever I'm not looking. I have to have eyes in the back of my head.

I wish I had the courage to kill him. I've been reading about a local woman called Mary Ann Cotton. She poisoned a number of husbands and their children. She used arsenic, which was, in those times, used to clean mattresses to kill bugs. No one suspected her because it was quite normal for women to purchase arsenic. In the book, she is painted as wicked, but who knows what indignities and atrocities she had to endure at the hands of her husband? Arsenic isn't something a housewife would buy today, but antifreeze is. Rat poison is. I have suffered more than anyone ever should.
Alice

Letter number thirty-seven
Dear Bertie,
He is dead at last. I have become every inch the grieving widow. They all sympathise. Even the Mister and Missus called and offered their condolences. I offered them tea. Were you not betrothed to another, we could have now been together at last. My whole adult life has been a living hell, thanks to him. I wish you health, wealth and happiness as I have always done. I couldn't bring myself to give away the child, so I must bring her up as my own, and one day, I might learn not to hate her.
Yours,
Alice

Letter number thirty-eight
Dear Bertie,
I've just heard the news of your death. I don't think I have any feelings left to be hurt. It was merely like the end of another chapter. The closing of a door. May you be in heaven half an hour before the devil knows you are dead.
Yours,
Alice

So, my father is dead. I will never have the chance to meet him. Perhaps my brother is still alive, though. I reread Mother's last letter. It's a letter to me.

Letter number thirty-nine
Dear Roberta,
Now you know my story. What I suffered, what I withstood, what I did and what I became. Try not to judge me too harshly. Remember the quote about walking in another's shoes. I bore so much, but when I saw the same disdain in his eyes directed towards you, I could not rest. How long would it have been before he turned his violence on you? As soon as you could speak, you would oppose him. Robert Gallbreath was not a man who would stand disagreements. I have presented as a very selfish woman, but that came later. You must understand that my only wish was to protect you. He always sided with Felicity. Even when she was very wrong. Especially when she was very wrong. He used you to hurt me.

I know that you've been affected. I wasn't a loving mother. I had no love left to give. All I had was pain. You may do what you wish with the information you have. I hope that you use it to form a bond with your children and try to love them as I should have loved you. By the time I realised what I had done, it was too late. The wall was there, and I couldn't break it down. Find Michael. Your other half. He might help to complete you in the same way that my twin completed me. I became half a person when I lost him.
Yours,
Mother

#headinthesand

This can't be true. Maybe it is some kind of cruel, sick joke. Mother's last jibe. Yet, it explains her coldness. I can't believe how much she lost. The pain she must have withstood.

There have been in the past, many times, when in temper, I could have cheerfully choked Knobhead. I could have run him over in my car, thrown rocks at him, stabbed him with my fork because of the hurt he caused me, but I can't imagine what my mother must have gone through. No wonder she was so cold and hard. This is way too heavy for me to deal with right now. I need to forget about it. Put it away and deal with it later. Maybe.

Chapter 15

#audaciousex

I have fifteen missed calls and three texts saying, 'CALL ME' in capitals from Mick. He must really want me to remove the photo of my kids from the office. I can understand why. They're not the most aesthetically pleasing individuals.

I'm sitting eating Haagen-Dazs in the middle of the day and thinking about cracking open a bottle of Shiraz when the doorbell dings. There's supposed to be a dong, but it's malfunctioning. Story of my life. I open the door and see the person I least expect to see.

He stands there in all his creased Calvin Klein glory. Knobhead. My ex-husband. I just stare at him. 'Hi, Roberta. Can I come in?' I'm still staring. 'Please, Roberta, I don't want to talk on the doorstep.'

'I don't really want to talk at all,' I manage.

'Roberta, have a heart.'

'Are you kidding me?'

'Please.' He looks like he's going to cry, so I open the door and walk back into the house. He follows me like a puppy that has been repeatedly kicked and is expecting another. *Don't tempt me.*

'Can I sit down?'

'I dunno, can you?'

He sits. He looks at me and shakes his head, then, to my horror, he bursts into tears. There's a whole garbled spiel, and I don't understand a word of it. Against my better judgement, I offer him a cup of tea and ask him to tell me slowly.

He sips at the scalding brew and starts to tell me again, swiping tears from his red eyes.

'I should never have done it. Left you, I mean. I should never have cheated on you with Terri-Ann…'

'…from Thomas Cook. Bit late to be thinking about that now… It's been sixteen years.'

'I know, I know, I'm a fool.'

'You won't get any argument from me.'

'The thing is, she led me astray with her see-through tops and crotchless panties.'

'Oh, so, it's her fault for being desirable as opposed to me who is–'

'No, no, you misunderstand. My head was turned by her, and we weren't…well…you know–'

'Having sex? Making love? Oh, yes, we weren't. Remind me, why was that now? Oh, because I was going through the whole sexual harassment thing at work. Pardon me for not giving you your quota of blow jobs during what was an extremely difficult time for me.'

'Sorry, this isn't coming out very well.'

'Again, no argument.'

'I realise now what a mistake it was.'

'So, you realise now, after you break my heart, upset the children, ruin my finances, marry another woman, and she bears your child. How old is Ruby again?'

'I love Ruby, but Terri-Ann…she can be so–'

'It's always someone else's fault, isn't it? It was my fault you cheated with Terri-Ann from Thomas Cook because I wasn't fulfilling your needs. What's wrong? Has she stopped putting out?'

'I wish you wouldn't call her that. She hasn't worked for them for years. She's manager at Lunn Poly now.'

'Why don't you get away, then?'

'Don't be like that, Roberta.'

'What do you want, Andy?'

'I want us to try again.' Speechless. Me. Dumbstruck. 'I know it could work. I'm not the man I was. I've changed.'

'Unless you've changed into another person entirely, then I'm not interested.'

'Just think about it. Promise me, you'll just think about it.'

'And what about Terri-Ann from...whatever travel agents she's working for at the mo?'

'She's history.'

It dawns on me. 'She's kicked you out, hasn't she? You've got nowhere to go, have you? That's why you came around here, isn't it? You stinking, low-life, dirty, fuck-ugly douche bag.' Every insult is accompanied by a slap to the upper body and face. He cowers like the cowardly twat he is. 'Get out of my home.'

'Technically, it's my house too. Remember, I still paid the mortgage up until the kids moved out, and the deed of trust states I have a share.'

'It's a very small share.'

'But I could force a sale. Unless, of course, you'd like to buy me out.'

'You piece of shit.' Another blow.

'Come on, Roberta, be reasonable. I just need a place to stay until I get myself sorted. I promise you I'll be out of your hair in a couple of months.'

'Your promises are like dried dog shit. You'll be gone in two weeks, or you'll have my Kurt Geigers up your jacksie.'

'Deal.'

***

I first met him in a bar. He was the ex of a new friend. She warned me to stay away from him, that he was a "user" and "a player", but I wouldn't hear of it. I thought it was sour grapes. She didn't want him, she was already married to Colm Finnegan, but she didn't want anyone else to have him. She didn't want him to be happy.

He was witty and charming. He was all those clichés. Tall, dark and handsome. Mother hated him, of course, but Mother hated everyone. Including me. He came and picked me up on his motorbike one day and took me to the seaside for fish and chips. He made my heart race and my legs go weak.

We pulled up outside the chippy, he took off his helmet and shook his shoulder-length curly hair free, his eyes twinkled, and I wanted him to kiss me more than I'd ever wanted anything. Instead, he wiped my cheek and said, 'Cod or haddock, Robbie-erta?' I wasn't hungry, I was horny.

'Just a cola for me,' I said.

As we snaked our way to the front of the queue, the smell tantalized my nostrils, and I found I was hungry after all. Too stubborn to say, I was relieved when he ignored my wish for no food and bought me cod and chips. We ate them on the sea front as the sun set, and the waves crashed against the shore. I had never been so happy. We fed the seagulls with the leftovers and dipped our toes in the freezing water. Full and happy, we ran hand in hand to the amusements and fed two pence pieces into the noisy machines. We left laughing and skipping back to the bike. By the time he dropped me at my door, I was desperate for him to kiss me. He patted my head like I was some kind of cute puppy, blew me a kiss and rode off into the night.

The next time he picked me up, we went to the pictures to see *Octopussy*. Mother would have killed me if she'd known I was riding pillion. I could just imagine her slapping me around the head and screaming, 'I didn't bring you up for fifteen years to have you killed on the back of a motorbike.' I sneaked out and had him pick me up two streets away so the nosy neighbours wouldn't report back.

I don't remember much about the film as I spent the whole time holding my breath, the sexual tension was so strong. I'd decided if he hadn't kissed me by the end of this date, I would kiss him. My hands shook at the thought, and my stomach churned.

When he dropped me that night, he insisted on walking me to my door in case something terrible happened to me. I pulled him into the garages on the estate and stuck the lips on him. When we came up for air, he was smiling.

'Steady on, Robbie-erta. I'm not that kind of guy.' We spent the next hour and twenty minutes playing tonsil tennis. I was late home, and Mother beat me with her shoe, but I didn't care. I was floating on air. He started picking me up regularly. I never knew when he was coming. I spent a year in a permanent state of expectation. When he didn't come, I was crushed, and when he did, I was the happiest girl in the world.

He proposed on Christmas morning when I was sixteen. I wore the ring for four months before I dared to tell Mother. She said, 'You better not be pregnant, my girl, or I'll leather ye.' I wasn't pregnant, but soon after we were married, my periods stopped, and I realised I was to be a mother before my seventeenth birthday.

Everything was fine. Two more children followed. I was a good and loving mother, he was a doting father, and then, he changed. I can almost pinpoint the exact time. He became sarcastic and never missed an opportunity to put me down. We stopped having sex because I was having a really difficult time. I was being sexually harassed at work. Why couldn't he at least try to understand what I was going through? I was a young, sweet, innocent little thing, and I'd been working for Toodles for a few weeks when Gavin

Coombes, the manager, started to come and stand behind me, telling me what a good job I was doing of typing the memos and filing the paperwork. I smiled and thanked him. Little did I realise he would see this as encouragement to go further. The next time, he put his hand on my shoulder, and then, it was close to my breast. I wriggled away because it made me uncomfortable. I didn't tell anyone because I thought it was my fault. I thought I must have encouraged him somehow. He stood behind me one day massaging my shoulders, and I told him to stop.

'Come on now, you know you like it,' was his response.

'I don't,' I said. 'I'd like you to stop.' The whole of the next week I couldn't do anything right. He would fling things under my nose and tell me to type them again. And again. Nothing was good enough. Then, he caught me in the stationery cupboard and put his hand up my skirt. I punched him in the face and that's when I lost my job.

Knobhead seemed to be supportive, but when I look back, it was all male bravado and guilt. He threatened to punch Coombes's lights out and bought me gifts: flowers, chocolates, jewellery… I should have known from the aftershave and the working late he was playing away. It was all textbook, but I was so young, so trusting, not to mention busy raising three small children. I had no experience of relationships. I thought this was what was supposed to happen after a few years.

When he dropped it on me, he just came out with it. We were eating chips and pork chops, brown sauce on the side and tea in a teapot. I was bustling round the table, plump with contentment.

'I'm leaving you,' he said. My mouth opened, but no words came out. I couldn't move. It was like I was frozen in time. 'I've met someone.'

'An affair?' I eventually managed, slumping into a chair. 'You've been unfaithful?'

'No. Not an affair. I'm in love. I'm leaving you. We were...'

'What? What were we?' I shouted, fists clenched. Anger burned within me.

'A mistake,' he said.

He got up, then packed his bags while I threw things and screamed. When that made no difference, I pleaded and begged. I clung to him as he kicked me away like I was an unwanted dog. I was numb. Bereft. In total shock. I couldn't believe it. We were so happy. So, in love. How could he do that to me? I wanted to kill her. I couldn't believe that he had fallen for someone else, that he was living with someone else, that he loved someone else. He was mine. We were supposed to last forever. He stood at the altar and swore to love and honour me, in front of all our family and friends. How could he just have taken up with a tart of a travel agent?

I rang and threatened them at regular intervals. I found out where she lived and turned up at the house. I smashed up her car, broke in to her house and filled all his shoes with cement. I was arrested three times. At the time, I felt like I was going mad. I obviously suffered a breakdown. I couldn't handle the pain, the loss and rejection. After that, I turned off my feelings to protect myself. Some women throw themselves into motherhood when this happens. Some throw themselves at other men. I did neither. I closed myself off from life, from people. I refused to be hurt again, so, for a while, I refused to live.

The all-encompassing love I'd had for Andy turned into the most rancorous hatred, which I aimed at everyone else.

Chapter 16

#sexpestilence

I take a selfie at breakfast and immediately delete it because Knobhead is in the shot.

I have ten missed calls from Mick and a text to say, 'Stop being so stubborn.' I'm still hurt, confused and angry about the work situation, and I'm in a state of disbelief that Knobhead is in the process of moving his stuff in.

'You're staying for two weeks, Andy. You don't need your Welsh dresser.'

'I can't leave it there. Terri-Ann has threatened to burn it.'

'Put it in storage, then. You can bring your clothes, and that's all.'

'What about my La-Z-boy?'

'And that's all.' It would be better than having his stinking carcass on my furniture. 'You're in the spare room, and I swear to God, if you go a-wandering during the night and end up in my bed at any point, I will do a Bobbit on you.' He knows this is no idle threat. I think he'll keep himself to himself.

#rainingmen

I take a selfie of me having breakfast: croissants and fruit, smoked salmon and hollandaise sauce. I think it makes me look like I'm holidaying in Europe. I add a filter and upload it to Facebook, Twitter and Instagram because it doesn't show my crow's feet and my teeth look white. I make it my profile pic and get two likes immediately: Johnathan the Foetus and Annie One-Eye from accounts. I have no missed calls or texts from Mick. He must've realised I'm not coming back. So why do I feel disappointed? I suppose it's like when you have a scab. You pick it off, you miss it.

Another weird email pings into my inbox. They're intriguing me, but that's what these viruses do. I resist the temptation to open it. "I exist in two places, here and where you are", the subject line says.

It's got to be easier tracing long-lost relatives now we have the internet. I type in "tracing a long-lost relative" and a number of sites pop up. I click on one of them, and it immediately asks for money. While I don't mind paying to find my brother, I'm sure there are companies that do it for free. I've heard of people who've done it on Facebook, so I could try that too.

I eat a family-sized bag of cheese and onion crisps and get raging indigestion. I consume twenty small doughnuts to see if that will help. It doesn't.

Never in a million years did I imagine I'd be cooking for Knobhead and chatting about the election. He pours me a glass of orange juice as I stir the béchamel.

'This is very civilised,' he says.

'Well, don't get too cosy,' I say. 'Two weeks, maximum.'

There's a knock at the door, and I ask him to get it as the sauce is at a crucial moment. I'm not going to have him telling everyone I'm a disaster in the kitchen as well as everywhere else. I hear a man's voice I recognise, but it's out of place, and I can't think to whom it belongs. I round the corner of the kitchen and see him. I nearly drop the saucepan. 'Roberta,' he says.

'Mick…er…this is Andy… I…my…husband…ex… husband.'

'I was worried,' Mick says. 'But I can see I had no cause to be. I wanted to try to set up a meeting to try and get you back to work.'

'Back to work?' I say in shock.

'Yes. I can see now that that's the farthest thing from your mind. I'm sorry to have interrupted you. I'll see myself out.' He disappears as quickly as he'd appeared, and I would have thought it was a dream but for the fact that Knobhead won't shut up about it.

'What does he mean, back to work? You on the sick?'

'No. I resigned.'

'Why does he want you back, then?'

'Oh, I dunno, Andy. Maybe he thinks I'm good at my job. Now, isn't that a novel idea? Me being good at something.'

'Roberta, you were good at lots of things.' He gives me a knowing wink, and I want to vomit. 'Maybe he fancies you.'

I look at him incredulously. 'He most definitely does not. We can't stand each other.'

'I'm telling you. He wants a slice of Robbie-erta.' He laughs.

'It's not completely ludicrous that someone would fancy me, and don't call me that.'

'Why? Does it bring back memories?' In truth, it does. Memories of when we were courting. Lazy days on Blackpool beach and back to the B and B for a night of passion. It had all been so simple then. Such fun. Then, he ruined it by getting married, having kids and breaking my heart.

'Memories you spoiled by shagging Terri-Ann from Thomas Cook.'

'Do you have to always bring that up? Can't we call a truce?'

'The truce has already been called, or you would not have your stinky DNA all over my bathroom and spare bedroom. I have to pop up to Durham after work to pick up Mother's ashes. I might stay over, so you'd better behave while I'm away. No wild parties.'

'Pinkie promise,' he says. 'What kind of arsehole would I be to be throwing wild parties at your place when you've just lost your mother?'

'What kind, indeed?'

#caughtshort

I decided not to stay at Mother's. If the truth be known, I felt a bit creeped out about staying in her house on my own. What if her spirit decided to wander? The journey home was a sober affair. It didn't feel right somehow to be quaffing Prosecco while Mother had been reduced to something that resembles cat litter. Felicity said she'd contact me about the will after we'd split the ashes. It didn't sit well with me, having Mother in two different pots, so I suggested to Felicity that we should get together to hold a little ceremony, and I left after an air kiss and an empty promise to write.

I get a short text from Mick saying he hopes I'm ok.

When I shove open my front door, I feel drained and emotional. I'm even looking forward to a bit of company as I watch *Corrie*. I cannot believe the sight that meets my eyes. Knobhead on my sofa, Calvin Kleins round his ankles, rutting away at some poor cow with her legs akimbo, her blonde bun bobbing up and down like a duck at the fair.

'Out,' I scream. 'Get out of my house.' It's only when she jumps up and grabs for her knickers that I realise who she is.

'Not so perfect now, eh, Pamela? Wonder what Steve will have to say about this.'

'You're not going to tell him, are you?' Fear fills her eyes. 'He'll kill me and Andy.'

'Two birds with one stone,' I say. 'Now get out of my house.'

Chapter 17

#swinglow

Today feels flat. An anti-climax without the climax. Job hunting is the order of the day. I update my CV and ping it off to a number of companies, then wait for the deluge of job offers.

Perhaps the menopause is responsible for the low mood. People might say, 'You've just lost your mother, it's to be expected.' But, to be honest, I never had her. She was never a mother. Not in the proper sense of the word. There were no hugs, no kind words, no soft stroking and storytelling. She kept us clean and fed, and we had a bed to sleep in. She was the first to admit she didn't have a maternal bone in her body. And yet, according to the letters, she had been maternal. She had loved us as much as it's possible to love, but when she lost my brother, she gave up on love.

'Why have kids?' I asked her one day.

'It's not like I had a choice,' she said. 'Contraception wasn't available until the sixties and obey wasn't just a word in the marriage service, it was a very real situation. If I had my time again, I'd have no kids.'

I now realise the hurt she went through and why she said those things. All I feel now is a deep, pervading sadness. I used to wonder how she could say she wished she'd had no kids, but now, I understand. If she hadn't had us, she would never have had to feel the pain of my brother's loss. And what agony that must have been. It was bad enough to lose a cheating husband but to suffer the loss of a child… When I was young, I think I associated her "black moods" as we called them with the death of our father. When I looked back as a teenager, I assumed she was grieving for him. If only I'd known she was mourning the loss of her child. If only she'd talked more. If I'd known she was dying, maybe I would have had time to make amends. Anger at Felicity flashes within me, but it burns out almost as soon as it begins. Like the flare of a match.

The man we thought was our dad, but who was apparently only Felicity's dad, had died when I was six, but I remember him being a big, warm bear of a man who smelled of menthol and had stubble. Mother always said I was viewing him through rose-tinted spectacles, and I never knew what she meant because I didn't wear glasses. I feel cheated now I realise he wasn't a good man but a tyrant. Someone much worse than Knobhead. My hurt pales into insignificance compared with the torment Mother must have gone through. I know I'm only getting one side of the story, but Mother was nothing if she wasn't honest. Brutally honest to the point of being completely tactless. And the letters are proof. Part of me wishes I'd never read them, but another part of me wants to understand Mother. Maybe in understanding her, I'll be able to have a much deeper understanding of myself. As it stands, I have a feeling that Sigmund Freud himself couldn't work me out.

I suppose I got my mothering skills, or lack of them, from her. I wasn't one of those earth mothers who threw on an apron and did potato painting. No glitter-glue or hugging trees in my house. At least that's how it became. I used to take my holidays during term time and arrange childcare during the breaks. They were clean, well fed and educated. Not that you'd think so now. Drew looks like a pot-smoking parasite (his looks do not belie the truth), Shoni hasn't got the sense she was born with when it comes to men, and Carolyn… Well, Carolyn's done alright. I suppose that's why they say she's the favourite.

I do love them. I do. I just find it difficult to show my emotions. There are times when I find myself wanting to give them a hug and tell them I love them, but I always stop myself. Love is pain. I wonder whether Mother felt the same way? You'd have thought on her deathbed she might have shown me some affection. Even if she couldn't bring herself to hug me, you'd have thought she could have brought herself to tell me she loved me. Then, it springs at me without warning. I should have told her. I should have said, 'I love you, Mam.' Why didn't I say it? Why? Love is pain. Guilt and heartache. Anger is easier to deal with so that's what I let it become. Just like Mother.

***

Knobhead's belongings are posted to him out of the bedroom window while he shouts from my small patch of lawn in the rain to "be reasonable". There's a satisfying smash as the photo of him with George Best hits the deck. I post a selfie of me with George Best and the caption, "Revenge: a dish best served with the smashing of your ex's favourite pic". It gets forty-eight likes in two minutes.

I receive a Facebook message from Harry. Would I like to meet for dinner? I've nothing better to do, so I message back. 'Ok.'

He lols me and says, 'Don't sound too enthusiastic.' There's something about men lolling that gets right on my nerves. It's up there with turnups on jeans and man buns, but I'm at a loose end, and one more evening alone in front of the telly might just send me over the edge, so I agree to meet him in the Dog and Duck for pre-dinner drinks. Big mistake. Huge.

#hangoverfromhell

Oh, God, I am dying. My head will not move from the pillow, but my stomach wishes to be rid of its contents. Why did I suggest the Dog and Duck? Why?

When I got there, Harry had already been joined by Mick, Tammy, the Foetus and the giggling girls from HR. 'We're joining you for dinner,' Tammy said. 'Isn't that nice?'

'Lovely,' I said sarcastically.

I had to sit through Mick's evil looks, Tammy's inane chatter about cunnilingus with the Foetus and tales of her homicidal brother who's in Strangeways for trying to bite off the nipple of a nightclub bouncer. Shoot me now.

I got very drunk. Plastered. No, drunker than that. Paralytic pretty much sums it up. My speech went first, which is probably just as well because in my head I was telling them all exactly what I thought of them. It wasn't pretty. Lucky that Tammy misunderstood when I called her a paedo and thought I was asking her to pass the dips.

'Quido? Is that what it's called? I thought it was guacamole.' She's such a tit.

A hot flush descended, and I had to take some air. I was standing with the smokers, trying to stay upwind, when Mick slithered up to me and grabbed my elbow.

'You're really something, Roberta.'

'Why, shankyou velly much.'

'That poor husband of yours.'

'Shay wha'?'

He shook his head like a disappointed uncle. What is wrong with that bloke? What the hell did he know about Knobhead? Poor husband, indeed. He must've heard that I'd thrown him out and about the whole perfect Pamela fiasco. How embarrassing. How dare he judge me? The last thing I remember is giving him a piece of my mind.

So here I am now, dying. I have no idea how I got home or, worse still, who undressed me and put me to bed. I pull the covers up and am preparing to have a duvet day when the phone rings. Felicity's face graces my screen. She's FaceTiming me. Oh fuck. Ordinarily, I would ignore it. Why I don't is beyond me. I press 'Accept', and the screaming starts.

'I knew it. I knew you and her were planning to do this. All those years wasted. All for nothing. Nothing. You two-faced, scheming, back-biting bitch.'

'Morning, Felicity.'

'How could you do this to me? Evil, both of you. I hope you rot in hell.'

'If you'd like to explain what's upset you so much…'

'Explain? You know fine well. Don't play the innocent with me.' The wails climb higher and higher. 'All those wasted years. I could have been in Bermuda with a husband. A police officer and respected member of the community. You bitch. I'll see you in court.'

My head pounds, my ears ache. I have no idea what she's talking about. When the bed stops spinning, I might try to find out.

I get a text from Mick asking, 'Are you alright?' And another saying, 'Nice arse' and a smiley face. Oh, God, what does that mean? I don't reply.

#wheretheresawill

The bed finally stopped spinning, my guts are empty, and my head feels like it belongs to me again. Turns out Mother has left everything to me in her will. I didn't think she had anything, except the house – a small terrace in a mining village in Durham in a very sorry state of repair. I'll be lucky to get sixty grand for it. And, of course, I would have split it with Felicity, but I've found out what she did.

It transpires Mother had a number of insurance policies and an investment account holding a pretty sizeable sum. Apparently, there was a payout when Dad died, and she hadn't touched a penny. It seems I am to inherit two hundred thousand pounds.

I know. I can't believe it, either. The terms of the will stipulate that I am not to share with Felicity, and I quote Mother, '…because she's a two-faced, lying, cheating, manipulative little bitch, and at least with you, what you see is what you get.' Ooh, Mother, talk about a sting in the tail and a backhanded compliment. No wonder Felicity's so angry.

Like I said, I would have given my "sister" half anyway. I really would, but the next revelation from Mother makes my blood fizz and my heart pound.

'Felicity, I know you took Bertie's watch and got your friend to sell it, pretending to be Drew. You knew how much it meant to me because of who it belonged to. That was such a spiteful thing to do. I could have forgiven that. Possibly. But what I can't and won't forgive, and I hope it haunts you for the rest of your days, is the fact that my Drew went through hell because of the accusations, and I go to my grave not having seen him because of you and your poison.'

That's what Mother had been trying to tell me in the hospital. Felicity had taken the watch and blamed Drew. What a bitch. The low-life, scheming, double-dealing, perfidious, pernicious bitch. Why would she do that to Drew? Jealousy. For some reason, Mother liked Drew. We're talking about a woman who didn't like herself half the time, but she had a soft spot for Drew. Felicity was jealous and wanted to ruin their relationship. That had to be it. She'd succeeded too. Drew was a pretty good suspect because of the shoplifting, the taking of phones from the other kids at school and the "borrowing" of the bingo winnings.

'I would never do that to Gran,' he'd said. And I'd half believed him. Only half.

Mother would get her wish. Felicity wouldn't see a penny of that money. Drew would. On the understanding that he didn't smoke it, drink it or shag it.

#mutinyandbounty

I ring Shoni to tell her I'll pay for the wedding. She can have a budget of twenty thousand and a designer dress. She sounds choked and won't stop thanking me.

'Give over with your mushy stuff,' I say.

I ring Drew and tell him I'll buy the catering van he wants. He can't believe it. There are even tears in his voice.

Then, I ring Carolyn to say I'll fund her PhD. She is actually speechless. For a full two minutes, she doesn't say a word, and then, she bursts into tears.

I have a funny, warm feeling I don't think I've had for a very long time. So, this is what it feels like to be nice. I quite like it.

Chapter 18

#normalservicehasbeenresumed

I hate everyone today. The hot flushes are at their worst, and my mood swings are swinging like a couple of middle-aged…well…swingers.

Being at home doesn't suit me. There's only so much *Jeremy Kyle* and *Cash in the Attic* one can stand without screaming at the telly. There's a woman on Jezzer today who is taking a lie detector to prove she didn't sleep with her daughter's transgender girlfriend. I get a mental picture of Lisa, Carolyn's girlfriend, and I'm a bit sick in my mouth. I switch over and watch an old re-run of *Abbot and Costello.*

I miss a call from Mick. What does he want? Probably to deride me for being drunk the other night.

I also have a Facebook message from Harry saying, 'Where did you get to lol?' So, if he hadn't taken me home and undressed me, who had?

I suppose I should call into work and pick up my stuff. I had better ring Tammy first to make sure I wasn't too out of order the other night before I show my face.

'Hi,' she says. 'You feeling better?'

'Yeah,' I say. 'What happened?'

'Think you had a little bit too much to drink.'

'Yeah, I think my drink was spiked.'

'Really? God, that's terrible.'

'So, how did I get home?'

'No idea. Jonathon and me decided to have an early night.' She giggles.

'Jesus, Tammy, is he not a bit too young?'

'For what?'

'For you.'

'You're as young as the man you feel.' She giggles again, and I want to slap her.

'Whatever turns you on.'

'Exactly,' she says.

'I was thinking about coming into the office today to collect my things.'

'What things?'

'Just some personal items. Things I had on my desk.'

'Oh, yeah, the bitch mug and the photos. I think Mick threw them, but I might be wrong.'

'He better not have. He's no right to touch my belongings.'

'Why don't you come at lunchtime, and we can go out somewhere? Jonathon's on a course, so I'm at a loose end.'

'Oh, well, when you put it like that.'

'I didn't mean…I mean, you'd have been welcome to join me anyway…I just meant…'

'Whatever, Tammy. I'll see you soon.' That girl makes my brain hurt, but she's the closest thing I have to a best friend so…

#tearsandfears

Mick's out with a client when I get to the office, so I text him to say I'm there to collect my personal effects. That makes it sound like I've died. He texts me to say he'd had them removed, but he'll bring them to the pub when he gets finished where he is.

Lunch turns into an afternoon drinking session, and at teatime, Mick joins us. He arrives at the pub clutching a small cardboard box containing the contents of my desk drawer. Twenty-five years with the company amount to a small number of obscure items that would fit in a much smaller shoebox. I plonk them on top of the bin and leave before I cry.

What's with the deluge of tears? It must be yet another middle-age thing. I only have to look at a picture of a puppy and I get pricks like nettle stings at the back of my eyes. I can't even stand dogs. What on earth is going on?

Mick sends a text saying, 'Hope you're ok.' Sarcastic bastard.

#hairtoday

I check in the mirror for facial hair. There's still no moustache, but I seem to be breeding a monobrow. I feel slightly relieved about the hairy lip situation and book an eyebrow wax at Saks.

Shoni rings to say they've set the date for the wedding and had the invitations printed. Do I want her to WhatsApp a pic? I really couldn't give a flying fox what the invitations look like, but my newfound bid to be nice has taken over. 'That would be lovely.'

When I open the picture, it takes a while to load. I think I'm looking at something else when the photo finally clears, and I can see it properly. A pink, fluffy, flamingo-like thing sits there. This can't be it, surely? It looks like something Katie Price would wear on her boobs.

'Very nice,' I message back. 'Very tasteful.'

'You being sarcastic, Mother?' is the response I receive. How come I can't be nice without people thinking I'm being sarcastic? What is that about?

If these are the invitations, I'm dreading seeing the dress.

'G2G am having my brows waxed.' It's not a lie. I'm just neglecting to tell her I'm having them waxed tomorrow.

#bridezillabombardment

I wake up feeling like I've been punched all over. My head hurts, my throat hurts, my elbows and knees hurt. I feel like my body has been poisoned. Waves of nausea wash over me. I want to just stay in bed and weep. Surely this can't all be down to middle age? I delete the selfie I've taken as I look as rough as toast.

Bridezilla texts to say the venue is decided for the wedding: Hardwick Hall. I promise myself I will complain about nothing. I will let her enjoy the organisation of and run up to the wedding. After all, it's downhill after that. Especially when you're marrying a drug dealer from Dagenham.

Drew texts to say his burger van has arrived, and he's spent the last four hours cleaning it. He's applied to the council for a pitch, and he's just waiting to hear. He's hoping to get a spot on the riverside, but they're sought after, and it's usually a case of who you know or how much money you have.

Carolyn calls to ask if I plan to sell Mother's house.

'Why?' I ask.

'Because if I get a place on the PhD at Durham, I'll need somewhere to stay.'

'What about Lisa?' Everyone knows Lisa is Carolyn's girlfriend, and they've been living together for years. Why she doesn't just come out of the closet, I don't know. I'm not sure who she thinks she's fooling.

'She'll try and get a job in a school up there.' Lisa is a teacher. She teaches English in an inner-city comp. She needs a bloody medal, as far as I'm concerned. They might get thirteen weeks holiday a year but imagine teaching nine different nationalities in one class. Not to mention the back-stabbings and assaults. And that's just from the other staff.

'It'll require renovation,' I say.

'I'll pay you rent, of course,' she says.

'No need.'

'Bloody hell, Mother, what has got into you? Not that I'm complaining.'

'I should think not,' I say. 'I'll have a company go in and clean it. Then, it'll just need a lick of paint.'

'Thanks.'

'Got to go. I'm off to the beautician. Yes, I know she's got her work cut out before you say anything.'

'I wasn't going to say anything, Mother. Except thank you and I love you.'

Oh, there it is again. Tears pricking the back of my eyes. What is wrong with me? Why have I turned to mush? Rarely have I heard my children tell me they love me, but then, I don't tell them. I did when they were little. When I was rocking them in my arms and singing them to sleep. I'd kiss their smooth little foreheads and tell them I loved them to infinity and beyond. When Knobhead left and broke my heart, I changed. I tried my best not to feel love because love was painful.

***

The beautician asks if I want my top lip done while she's waxing my eyebrows.

'Do you think it needs it?' I ask in a panic. 'I didn't think it was that bad.'

'Personal preference,' she says.

What's that supposed to fucking mean? 'So, it doesn't need it?'

'It's entirely up to you.'

For Christ's sake. 'Take it off, then,' I say. Little did I realise how sensitive that area would be, never having had it done before.

'Jesus Christ, you nearly took my fucking teeth along with it,' I say.

'Pride's painful,' she says in that tinkly sing-song voice they all have.

It's painful on the purse strings too. I must find a job like that. One where I can inflict pain and get paid for it.

Another weird email arrives on my phone. "Let there be room in your togetherness and let the wind of change dance between you". I open it, but there's no content. I reply with, 'Who is this?' An email immediately bounces back telling me this is a 'no reply' address. I look back at all the others I've received and realise they all seemed to be hinting about my twin brother. Or am I just imagining that? Is it wishful thinking, knowing what I now know?

I Google how to find a long-lost relative, and the Salvation Army website pops up. I click on the link and it takes me to a page entitled Reuniting Families. There's an email address to send enquiries to so I email them, telling them what I know about my brother and asking for their help. I wonder what it would be like to have a brother. I spent my childhood wishing I had one, someone to look out for me, stick up for me, look after me, chase the bullies away. I longed for a brother, and now I know I had (or have) one, I desperately want to meet him. I'm excited at the thought of finding him, but anxious that I never will. What if he's dead already? What if he doesn't want to meet me? My mind is awash with questions.

Chapter 19

#terminaltemperature

I ring the doctors to make an appointment for this afternoon. I'm sure there's something seriously wrong with me. A person cannot feel this crap for no reason.

The doctor takes a pint or two of blood, then checks my blood pressure and my temperature. Both normal.

'Really? I'm burning up.'

'Not according to this,' he says.

'My joints burn too,' I say. He prints me off a prescription for Naproxen, Fluoxetine, domperidone.

'I'm gonna rattle at this rate. Shouldn't we find out what's causing the symptoms rather than just treating them?'

'I think we know what's causing the symptoms,' the doctor says.

'Do we?'

'We discussed the menopause at your last appointment.'

'Oh, so, because I'm middle-aged and possibly menopausal, I just have to put up with it: the sickness, the pain, the itching, the burning...'

'It happens to all women at your time of life.'

'Yeah, if it happened to men, I bet there'd be more research into it. I bet they'd have a cure for hot flushes by now.'

'Ms Gallbreath, I don't think that attitude is very helpful, do you?'

I don't think your prescription is very helpful, so we're even. I leave with threats to complain to the practice manager.

'You're welcome to do so. My wife is the practice manager,' he says.

Bollocks.

Bridezilla sends a photo of flowers and some annoying relation of the Drug Dealer from Dagenham in a peach "flower-girl" dress. 'Doesn't she look cute?' *She looks like flamingo sick* is not an acceptable and tactful answer, so I type, 'Yes.' I'm getting good at this being nice lark.

Mick texts to say my job has been left open for me and to get in touch if I want to reconsider my hasty decision. Cheek. The truth is, I am regretting my decision. I miss my job. It was one of the few things I was good at but there's no way I'm having Mick the Dick tell me what to do.

#feelingflaky

My skin doesn't belong to me anymore. It's not the skin I've known all these years. I have bumps and lumps, itchy red blotches, flaking patches. 'It's eczema and acne,' the doc says as though I should know and, worse still, should just accept it.

'Yes, but why?' I ask. 'I haven't had acne since I was a teenager or eczema since I was a small child.'

'It's the hormones,' he says. 'I'll give you a course of antibiotics and some hydrocortisone. Don't worry, it's perfectly normal. We'll take some bloods.'

Mick texts this afternoon to say he's left messages on my answerphone and I haven't returned his calls. It transpires that the answerphone isn't working properly. There's a message from the doctor asking me to call him urgently. Shit, it must be the results of my blood tests. Already? There must be something wrong. By the time I get to the surgery, I've worked myself up into a panicked frenzy. I'm imagining months of chemotherapy and becoming bald and skeletal. I made the mistake of Googling the symptoms and came up with all manner of horrible diseases from liver failure and uterine cancer to non-Hodgkin's Lymphoma.

'Roberta Gallbreath,' I say to the receptionist, expecting pitying looks and an offer of tea.

Instead, I get a brusque, 'Wait there,' while she disappears into the office behind reception. She returns clutching a small bottle. 'Doctor wants a urine sample.'

'Now?'

'Yes,' she says.

'I can't just bloody perform on demand.'

'Just pee in the bottle and hand it back in here,' she says, tutting and scribbling something on the side of the container. I stuff it in my bag before anyone can see what it is and promptly forget about it.

Another email pops up on my phone: "Not double the trouble but twice blessed". They're beginning to irritate me.

#happyfamilies

Carolyn and Lisa moved into Mother's today. Carolyn calls to say Felicity came around to rant and rave, but Lisa threw her out and told her not to come back unless she was prepared to speak civilly. I'm liking Lisa more and more. Though not enough to have an affair with her and end up on Jeremy Kyle, I must add. Drew texts to say he's got a pitch on the Quayside for his van and he's over the moon. Shoni WhatsApps me her seating plan. As if I give a monkey's who sits where, as long as I don't have to sit next to her father. I text her to say, 'Very good' and 'Looking forward to wedding.' This isn't a total lie as I'm looking forward to getting dressed up and drinking lots of gin.

My car makes a loud noise, and smoke emanates from the exhaust. A huge bang resonates through the neighbourhood. My neighbour thinks I've been shot and pokes her head over the wall.

'Oh, you're alive.' She sounds disappointed. Maybe my untimely death would have brought some excitement to her humdrum existence. 'There was a man here for you yesterday.'

'A man?'

'Yes. Queer looking sort. Knocked on my door by mistake. I said you was out. He said he'd call back later.'

'What did he look like?' I ask.

'Like he should be in prison or a loony bin.' I have no idea who that could be. She knows Andy, so it can't have been him. Mick hardly looks like he should be in Frankland. It couldn't be Drew because Mrs Jones knows him.

'Our local MP?'

'No, not 'im. Though that bugger should be in prison. If he calls again, I'll get his name.'

Julian rings. I suppose you could call us friends. We've hung around together over the years. He often comes and spouts his problems at me, but then disappears when I have problems that I'd like to offload.

It transpires his boyfriend has dumped him just before Pride. He wants to come round to analyse the situation. I can't think of a good enough excuse in time, so here he is, perched on my sofa, parleying about his problems.

Apparently, Dave has been a bit distant. In that he kept buggering off to Gran Canaria at the drop of a helmet. I said at the time there was something amiss, but Julian was all, 'We're soulmates, he wouldn't do that to me.'

I was all, 'He's a man, of course he would.' He said I was just a bitter and twisted feminazi because of what had happened to me, and you can't judge every man by Knobhead's standards.

Turns out Dave has been shagging a Liverpudlian holiday rep in Las Palmas.

'A scouser!' says Julian. 'I bet he's got chlamydia.' On the back of this, Julian had been to get himself checked out, and the doctor noticed he was having some worrying symptoms.

'He's suggested a colonoscopy,' Julian says.

'Sounds painful.'

'They stick a camera up your bum hole,' he says.

'Are you not worried about it?' I say.

'As long as they take the tripod off, I'm sure I'll be fine. Anyway, I need a night out,' Julian says, 'before I have to go into hospital. The Toon, baby. Tonight.'

'Newcastle on any night is my idea of hell: Mexican mariachi bands, giant blow-up bananas and gaggles of girls dressed as Princess Leia.'

'How can you refuse a friend who has…'

'Has what?'

'Well, we don't know what.'

'Has to have a camera shoved up his bum hole?'

'Exactly.'

'Oh, alright, but we eat first. Somewhere nice.'

So, we're sitting in McDonald's in The Big Market, because somebody "forgot" to book the restaurant and the queues for Jamie Oliver's and The Botanist were ridiculous, and who should walk in but Mick and all his work cronies.

'Bob, fancy seeing you here.'

'Fancy,' I say.

'Out on the town?'

'Looks like it.'

'Join us,' Julian says, and I could have punched him in the throat.

'Don't mind if we do,' Mick says, smirking at me.

'What a hottie,' Julian says when Mick goes to order his food.

'Are you freakin' kidding me?'

'No, he's a bit tasty.'

'Yeah, well, you like fast food, so there's no accounting for taste.'

'Is he…?'

'I dunno, you'll have to ask him. You have the worst gaydar of any gay man I've ever known.'

'He married? Kids?'

'No idea.'

'Not that that's always an indicator, cos I've known plenty of married men who help out when we're short. Be a good girl and put a word in for me.'

'My friend thinks you're cute,' I say when Mick returns from the counter balancing a tray and fumbling to stuff his change into a trouser pocket.

'Is this one of those things where people say their friend but really mean themselves?' says Mick. Told you he was a dick.

'Er, what do you think?'

'I think you haven't been able to take your eyes off me all evening.'

'And I think you talk out of a hole in your head.'

'Methinks you protesteth too much, Roberta dear.'

'Get lost.' I storm out, and Julian follows me.

'What did he say? He interested?'

'No, he's straight.'

'Damn. What a waste.'

An Asian taxi driver pulls up beside us and winds down his window. 'You want lift?'

'Yeah,' I say. 'Get us out of here.'

'We leaving your friends?' Julian asks.

'They're not my friends.' We jump in, and the driver pulls away.

'Been busy?' Julian asks him.

'Your girlfriend is stunning,' he says.

'Oh, she's not my girlfriend. She's single.'

I nudge him hard in the ribs, and he yelps.

'Where to?'

'Sinners,' Julian says.

'You're joking,' I say.

'I thought we could hit the karaoke bar and then go to The Loft in the gay village.'

'Sinners is the tackiest bar on the planet, and The Loft is the weirdest club in existence. Last time I went, I had my fanny bitten three times.'

'Come on, Roberta, live a little.'

When we get to Sinners, a sixty-year-old bald guy is singing "I Will Survive" while a stripper with bruises all over her thighs spins on a greasy pole.

'He won't survive for much longer if he doesn't shut up,' I say. 'I'm ready to put him out of his misery.'

'Killjoy,' Julian says. 'Come on, let's get into the spirit of it.' He orders a line of shots and downs them one after another. 'Your turn.'

Fifteen shots later and I'm on the mic with Julian singing, "I Am What I Am". Two hours and a couple of lap dances later (one by me and one for me), we leave Sinners and stand in line for The Loft. A girl with a lobster tattooed on her nose and a mullet perched on her head stamps our hands as we pay to get in. They should be paying me.

We're ordering tequila when Mick the dick and co arrive.

'Told you he was on my team,' Julian says.

'He isn't,' I say.

'Then what's he doing here?'

'Er, excuse me, *I'm* here.'

'Yeah, but you're with me and…'

'And he might be with a gay friend.'

'True, or he might be on the bi-bus.' Julian waves, and they stagger over. 'Roberta's pulled,' he says. Mick gives me a look of disgust. Where does he get off? 'The taxi driver, no less.'

'Great, you can blow him on the way home, so he'll waive the fare,' Mick says with ice in his voice.

I decide against that suggestion and sneak away alone, leaving Julian to leer over Mick and the Foetus.

#hangoverfromhell

Today is a terrible day. Menopausal hangovers are the worst. The hot flushes are like forest fires, and my head pounds relentlessly. I am never speaking to Julian again. It's all his fault.

I got home at five and was woken at six by a blank text from Mick. I have no idea what that was about. Maybe it was to tell me he's not speaking to me. He was particularly obnoxious last night. If he thinks I'm going back to work for him when he can't even be civil, he's got another think coming.

I down four Nurofen and two Panadol with a glass of orange juice. I retch and bring them all back up. I retire to bed for the day with a cold cloth and a bucket.

I eventually wake after a day of the DTs and have seven missed calls from Mick, two from Drew and one from Shoni. I'm too tired to ring people back. Julian sends a text to say, 'Good night. Btw you were right about Mick.'

Dear God, I hope this means he thinks I'm right about him being a dick and doesn't mean he tried it on with him. I hope Mick doesn't think I put him up to it. He probably does. That's probably what the missed calls are about. I'll just ignore them until he calms down.

Chapter 20

#flippingburgers

I lost two days of my life to a monumental hangover. Drew rings with a crisis and needs my help. He has an appointment with a supplier and needs me to man the van. Or woman the van, as the case may be. Me? Flipping burgers. Bloody Nora. So, it is my only son's fault I suffer the biggest humiliation of my life to date. That might be an exaggeration – there have been many degradations – but my face is still burning.

So, I'm there in the middle of Newcastle wearing a ketchup-stained white coat and hat, flipping burgers and smelling of onions. There is a queue from me to County Hall, and I am running out of white rolls. The heat is unbearable. A furnace. My face is lit up like a traffic light and sweat springs from every pore.

'Nice buns,' a voice says. Of course, who else but Mick the Dick?

I want to tell him to piss off, but there is a line of customers, and it won't look good. Drew will never forgive me if I ruin his big chance.

'What do you want?' I manage.

'Nine burgers, four hotdogs, one without mustard, one without ketchup, two without onions, or mustard, two cheeseburgers, five diet Cokes, four regular, one Dr Pepper...'

'Do you wanna say that again?' I say grabbing a pen and writing on the corner of a paper bag. How does Drew remember it all?

'Not really.'

I throw him one of my best looks.

'Oh, alright. Nine burgers, four hotdogs, one without mustard, one without ketchup, two without onions, or mustard, two cheeseburgers, five diet Cokes, four regular, one Dr Pepper, or was it four diet and five regular?'

'Are you kidding me?'

'The customer is always right, Bob.'

'A hundred and sixteen pounds and eighty-seven pence please.' I'm reaching into the bag for his change when everything moves. I can feel myself falling in slow motion, but there is nothing I can do to stop it.

When I wake up, I'm lying on the grass, my skirt past my knees and my blouse open. A man in green leans over me.

'Hello, Roberta. Can you tell me what day it is? Who's the prime minister?' I can't remember what day it is. They all roll into one when you're not working. And I can't remember the prime minister's name. Ineffectual, stuck-up little shite who went to public school and thinks benefits are something Daddy gets from the board. Name escapes me. Terrible haircut. If they ask me who Peter Andre is shagging or who won *Love Island,* I could tell them. As it is, they think I have concussion from the fall.

'She's delirious,' a voice says.

'She's sweating terribly.' Obviously never heard of the menopause, these fuckers.

'Better take her in. Would you like to come in the ambulance, sir?'

So, I'm sitting in the ambulance, hooked up to a drip, with Mick mopping my sweaty brow.

'Thought I was gonna have to give you the kiss of life there, Roberta.'

'God forbid,' I say.

He puts on this pathetic wounded look. 'Wouldn't be that bad, would it?' he says.

'I'd rather pierce my own nipples with a fish fork.'

'Normal Friday night for you, I should imagine.'

'Ooh, call the tailor to stitch up my sides.'

'Just relax,' says the man in green who I learn is called Dave. 'We're nearly at the hospital.'

'I really don't need to go to hospital. What about Drew's burger van?'

'Drew?' asks Mick.

'My boy–'

'Oh, your boyfriend. Just how many do you have, Roberta?' There's that fake wounded look again. I have one nerve left, and he's swinging on it.

'Hundreds,' I say. 'Not to mention the secret admirers.'

'Don't worry about your boyfriend's catering van.' I don't correct him. I don't want him to think I'm sad and single. 'Tammy is looking after it. She quite fancies herself as a burger tosser or whatever they're called. Have to say I thought you had more ambition than that.'

'Should've been you. You're an expert tosser,' I say, and I'm about to put him right about a few things when the ambulance lurches to a stop, and the paramedic opens the back doors.

'Right, you, let's be having you.' He drags me out, bumping me down a number of steps.

'I bet you don't get this if you go private. I bet Bupa doesn't feel like the bumper cars,' I say.

Dave ignores my protestations and wheels me into the manic A&E, dumping me on a trolley in a corridor saying, 'One more coming in, Barbara. This bitch bites.'

I shall be writing to my MP.

'I'm not lying here all day,' I say to Mick. 'If they haven't seen to me in ten minutes, I'm leaving.' I try to loosen the strap that has me shackled to the table. 'I feel like I'm at an S and M convention.'

'Damn, I left my gimp mask in the ambulance.'

'I'm sure you've got things to do,' I say.

'Not especially,' he says.

'I'll be fine on my own.'

'Wouldn't dream of leaving you,' he says. There was an awkward silence.

'Get me out of here,' I say.

'So bossy,' he says.

'Just do it.'

'Bloody hell, no wonder you were in line for a management position.'

'What?'

'Yeah, before you went shooting your mouth off and spitting your dummy out, they were going to offer you the job of office manager.'

I'm speechless, which is obviously very unlike me. He's probably lying to wind me up.

'So, would you consider coming back to work?'

'Why?' This must be some kind of trap.

'Just wondered. We miss you. I miss you,' he says.

'No one to take the piss out of?' I say.

'On the contrary, there's lots of people, but none so much fun as you.'

'I'll bet,' I say.

'How about coming back on Monday? If you're up to it.'

'Of course, I'm up to it. Why wouldn't I be?'

'You had a nasty fall this afternoon.'

'Nonsense, I just fainted because of the heat. I didn't even bang my head. I'm absolutely fine. I shouldn't even be here. I should be helping Drew.'

'So, you'll come back Monday?'

'I'll think about it,' I say. 'On one condition.'

'What's that?'

'That you take me home, right now.'

***

I can't even remember getting home. I wake alone to the beeping of my phone. I have a couple of abusive texts from Felicity which I delete and four missed calls from Mick. An insistent text tone reveals the message: 'I know you're there. Stop ignoring me. I have something to tell you.'

I switch off the phone and fall back to sleep.

I wake in a haze. When I switch on my phone, I have seven messages from Shoni. When I ring her, she's crying. 'He's gone, Mum.'

'Who?'

'Who'd you bloody think? Kevin.'

I thought it would be all my fault. 'Gone where?'

'I don't know. He's been acting strange, and when I woke up this morning, he'd gone. There was a note that said, "Don't try to follow me." Except I can't follow him, because I don't know where he's gone.' She wails, and I can hear her blowing her nose.

'Maybe it's for the best,' I say.

'How can it possibly be for the best?' she screams at me. 'You say the stupidest things. You have no understanding of anything. What kind of mother are you?' I'm aware she must have been talking on the house phone as I hear a slam as she cuts me off. I'll ring her later when she's calmed down.

Drew rings to ask if I'm ok, and when I say I'm fine, he berates me for leaving his beloved burger van.

'Lucky that Tammy did an ok job of cooking and selling, so my reputation isn't entirely ruined.'

So, what are you complaining about? is what I want to say. Instead, I say, 'Good. That's good.' I'm getting good at this biting my tongue lark.

#stillbitingmytongue

The receptionist from the doctor's surgery calls today. She says the doctor wants me to make an appointment, so she's made one for me for Monday. I've decided I'll go back to work. I ring Mick, and he invites me for a back-to-work meeting on Monday, so I'll have to cancel the doctor's appointment. It can't be anything important, or he'd have rung himself instead of getting the dragon to do it.

The menopausal symptoms are no better. I have a horrible metallic taste in my mouth, and I've gone off coffee and mushrooms. Even the sight of them on *MasterChef* makes me want to barf. The night sweats are getting worse, and I'm suffering from terrible headaches. What we women have to put up with is nobody's business. I wish I was through the other side. I must buy an electric razor.

I text Mick to ask for the number for HR as the one I have is going straight to voicemail. 'You don't need an excuse to get in touch' is his pathetic, juvenile response. Seriously, the man is a total douchebag.

Shoni rings to say the druggie from Dagenham is back safe and sound. Well, safe. I'm not sure how sound he is. He'd been to buy her a present, a proper engagement ring, which was why he said not to follow. She wants to know what I meant by my "maybe it's for the best" remark.

'I don't know,' I say. 'It's just one of those things that people say.'

'Maybe people should be more careful about the things they say in future,' she says.

'Believe me, I'm being very fucking careful.'

'What's that supposed to mean?' she asks. That girl is always spoiling for a fight.

'Nothing, Shoni. I've got to go. There's someone on the house phone.'

That's a lie, but then, the phone rings, and Carolyn say, 'There's a weird man keeps hanging round outside Grandma's house.'

I tell her to ring the police. You hear all sorts, don't you, about stalkers and weirdos doing away with people in their sleep. I tell her to change the locks, and she says she rang me for reassurance, but she now feels terrified to go to sleep.

'Thanks, Mother.'

There's no bloody pleasing some people.

Shoni rings again all sweetness and light (bloody schitzo) to ask if I think it's appropriate to ask Carolyn to be her bridesmaid. I say I think it's a lovely idea.

'You don't think I should ask Lisa, do you?'

'Not if you don't want to,' I say.

'I don't know what the protocol is for lesbian partners,' she says.

'I don't think there's a rule book.'

'I know that, Mother, but what's the *done* thing?'

'I think people pretty much do as they please these days.'

'That's good,' she says. 'Because I don't think she'd suit lemon Grecian.'

I say nothing.

The receptionist from the doctors' surgery rings again. I can tell by her voice it's Maria. Fat woman with a moustache and an arse that should have a "Danger wide load" sticker. I can't stand her.

'Mrs Gallbreath, Doctor Lambert…'

'It's Miss.'

'…has been trying to get in touch with you. He's rung you personally and left messages for you to get in touch.'

'My answerphone is broken,' I say.

'He's sent two letters.'

'Post must've been delayed.' I glance at the unopened mail on the hallstand.

'It's important that you make an appointment at antenatal.'

'For who?' Am I missing something? Is Shoni pregnant and didn't tell me? Why would she give my number?

'For you.'

'Why on earth would I need to make an appointment at antenatal?'

'Because your recent pregnancy test was positive,' she snaps.

'What pregnancy test? I haven't had a…' I remember the doctor asking for a urine sample. I can't remember him saying he was doing a pregnancy test. He might have done but… 'I can't be pregnant. I'm menopausal.'

'The blood test result indicates you are not through the menopause. Peri-menopausal woman can still get pregnant. Weren't you taking precautions?'

'I'm not sexually active,' I say. Well, I'm not. As a rule. There was only that night, but that was months ago. Dear God, no. NO. NOOOOOO.

'Really?' she says. 'Shall I put you down for two o'clock Wednesday?'

Chapter 21

#inshock

I'm in shock.

I'm too depressed to write, speak or eat.

And I'm still in shock.

I'm trying to get my head round this. The sickness. Not menopause. The headaches. Not menopause. The aching joints. Not menopause. The nausea. Not menopause. The fluttering's. Not IBS. PREGNANT!

Fucking pregnant!

To Mick the Dick!

The worst thing is, there's no way I can have a termination. The conference in Harrogate was five and a half months ago. What am I going to do?

I'm in bed. Feeling very sorry for myself. The phone keeps ringing. I'm ignoring it. Everyone on Facebook is "feeling blessed". I want to kick them until they can't move. Twitter folk are all counting their blessings. Piss off!

I'm not just fat. Blessing counted.

How could I not know? Sickness, nausea, going off coffee and mushrooms, headaches, flutterings, gaining weight, mood swings. How could I not know? Poxy doctor and his menopause theory.

I remember a previous conversation. 'Is there any chance, Roberta, that you could be pregnant?'

'None at all,' I said.

'You sure?'

'Certain. Unless it's the immaculate conception.'

Argh!

There was nothing immaculate about it. It was drunken, messy, disastrous and embarrassing.

#whatmenopause?

I'm too bloated and ugly to take a selfie. I have thousands of missed calls and texts. I'm ignoring everyone. I'm trying to ignore the door, but someone is being very insistent. I look through the spy hole and see Mick.

'Roberta, I know you're in there.' He cannot see me like this. I never want to see him again. 'Just open the door. Why didn't you come to work on Monday?'

Work. Shit. I forgot. I'm pregnant and insane. Depressed. Go away.

'I'm going to keep coming back and knocking on the door until you open up.'

Another battering on the front door and Tammy's voice says, 'Roberta, are you going to open this door, or am I going to knock it down?' *Really? Couldn't knock the top off a rice pudding.* 'I mean it, Roberta.'

'Go away.'

'I knew you were in there. Open the bloody door, will you? I'm freezing my tits off out here.'

'You didn't have any to start with.'

'Pleased to see you haven't lost your sense of humour along with your marbles.'

'Who's with you?' I ask.

'No one.'

'I don't believe you.'

'Christ, Roberta. Who do you think is with me? The SAS? Have you been smoking stuff?' I open the door, and she falls in. 'What the hell is the matter with you. Blooming stinks in here.'

'Charmed.'

'Open a bloody window.' She flings open the kitchen window, eyes the empty wine bottles and pizza cartons, tuts like a disapproving mother and runs hot water into the sink. 'I'm going to run you a bath, wash these dishes and clean this place up, and then, you're going to tell me what the hell is going on.'

***

I have never seen Tammy speechless. Never. Her mouth opens and closes like a dying fish. I'm sitting in a towel with another wrapped round my head while she does guppy impressions.

'Pregnant?' she eventually manages.

'That's what I said.'

'But when…how…who…where? Jesus!'

'Exactly. So, forgive me if I'm not dancing the hornpipe round a maypole in my undies.'

'Jesus.'

'You've said that.'

'How long… How many…?'

'Months? Weeks? Not sure but using my powers of deduction, I'd say five and a half months.'

'Christ in a four-wheel drive… Who?'

'I don't want to talk about that.'

'You never even said you were seeing anyone.'

'I wasn't.'

'Shit. A one-night stand?'

'Yep.'

'Who?'

'You don't know the guy.' Lies.

'I'm a bit miffed you didn't tell me.'

'Pardon me for not filling you in on all the gossip, but a bit miffed doesn't cover it for me. I'm a bit abso-fucking-lutely devastated.'

'I can imagine. Shit. I thought you were menopausal.'

'So did I. So did my poxy doctor. Apparently, peri-menopausal women can still procreate. Who knew?'

'Oh God! What have the kids said?'

I give her a look.

'Oh, you haven't told them. I don't envy you that task.'

'Really not helping, Tammy,' I say.

'Oh yeah, sorry. At least…er…'

'At least I'm not just getting fat?'

'Yeah. Every cloud…' she says. 'When are you going to tell them?'

'You gonna be there when I do?'

'Christ, no. I was wondering when to leave town. They are going to flip.'

'Cheers, friend.'

'What shall I tell Mick?'

'Mick? What's he got to do with anything? I don't know what you're insinuating about me and Mick, but I can assure you–'

'Calm down, Roberta. I just meant what shall I tell him about you not turning in for work? He knows I was coming here to see what's wrong with you.'

'Oh.'

'So, what shall I tell him?'

'Tell him I left the country. Tell him I have leprosy. Tell him I died.'

'I'll tell him you have flu.'

'Swine flu.'

'I'll tell him you'll be back Monday.'

I look at her.

'You'll need to come back. You'll need a decent maternity package.'

'Shit.'

Chapter 22

I'm not taking a selfie today. I have spots on my chin, greasy roots and a fat stomach.

I receive a text message from Mick saying, 'I hope u r ok.' Liar.

I need a distraction from the devastating news. I figure if my brother was adopted by the couple who wrote to my stepfather, his name would be Michael Rowbotham. I enter it on a Facebook search and get twenty-five hits. I start sending messages…

Against my better judgement, I'm attending an antenatal appointment. I'm sitting in a waiting room with girls young enough to be my grandchildren, feeling like an old beast of burden. A pregnant hippo. A hormonal cow. I've got my bra on the last fastener, and I've loosened the top button of my jeans, pulling the zip down halfway, but I still feel trussed up like a Christmas turkey.

'Urine sample,' Nurse Ratchet demands. She's broad and wears a hairnet over a tight bun. She looks like a Russian shot-putter (male). I hold out the small bottle I've been clutching. She disappears, and another nurse appears and invites me into a room to have my weight scrutinised and my height noted. I'm then shunted into a small room where a radiographer tries her best to make me piss myself. She squashes my bladder while trying to see the sprog.

'Can't seem to get a very good picture,' she says.

'Doesn't matter,' I say.

'Don't you want to see baby?'

'No.'

For the rest of the appointment, I'm treated like a pariah. Pardon me for not doing cartwheels round the corridors. I'm nearly fifty years old. I should be watching *Antiques Roadshow* and ordering a stairlift. Not procreating, changing nappies and having sleepless nights. I should be looking forward to Elton John concerts, dancing to Billy Ocean and developing a love of sherry; instead, I am facing a new generation of stretch marks and a knackered pelvic floor. What have I done to deserve this?

I could give the kid away. Take an extended break, give birth, have it adopted and come home. Nobody would be any the wiser. Or I could see this as a chance to put right all the wrongs of my previous parenting. I could get it right this time. Be a proper, loving mother who paints on the patio and plays with Play-Doh on rainy afternoons. The words of Mother's letter keep coming to mind. *Form a bond with your children and try to love them as I should have loved you*. Easier said than done.

I've sent Facebook messages to every Michael Rowbotham on the site but had no response yet. I still haven't had a response from the Salvation Army, but they have a special department that deals with reuniting lost family members, so they might be able to help.

I've invited the kids over for supper. I'm going to tell them about the pregnancy tonight. I'll tell them all at once and get it over with.

***

I could have predicted Shoni's reaction. She rants and raves for ten minutes about how selfish I am and how I just want to steal her thunder.

'I'm cancelling the wedding until you come to your senses,' is her parting shot before she storms out in a huff.
Drew shrugs and says, 'Whatever. Cool,' then has to dash as he has to get to the wholesaler to buy sesame seed buns.
Carolyn got the train from Durham. Cries. Real tears. For about half an hour. Then hugs me before jumping on the train home. My kids are weird.

***

Now, I'm sitting with Tammy watching crap TV and eating ice cream while she drinks wine. She's brought me a bottle of non-alcoholic red which is basically just grape juice. 'Thought you might like to feel as if you're having a drink,' she says.

'I might like to just have a drink,' I say.

'It's bad for the baby, though,' she says.

I take a couple of sips.

'Is it good?' she asks.

'Good would be an exaggeration,' I say. 'It's drinkable.' The flavour isn't bad, but it's not as moreish as normal red wine. 'Perhaps if I stick a shot of gin in it…'

'That kind of defeats the object, Roberta,' Tammy says when she sees what I'm doing.

'You're no fun. Give me a glass of that.'

'No, you're not allowed.'

'I've been pissed for the past five months – one glass of white wine's hardly going to hurt it further.'

'One glass,' she says, pouring a meagre measure. I take one sip and rush to be sick.

'Coffee, mushrooms and alcohol,' I say between bouts of vomiting. 'Sure-fire sign I'm pregnant.'

'Mick's been asking after you,' she says, coming to stand behind me and holding back my hair.

'Probably worried I won't come back, and he'll have to face the Carters on his own.'

'No, I think he's genuinely concerned. He's not all bad, Roberta. He can actually be quite nice.'

'Pah. You haven't got the hots for him, now, have you?'

'No, Jonathon and I are very happy, thank you. I'm just saying, Mick's not all bad.'

'Yeah, neither was Attila the Hun, and I'm sure Pol Pot had some fans.'

'What's Paul Potts got to do with it? Really, Roberta, you're being very random. Must be the hormones.'

'I was talking about dictators.'

'Who's he?'

'Who?'

'Dick Taters. Don't think I've met him. Is he that new guy in accounts?'

'Are you really as thick as you act, Tammy?'

'There's no need for rudeness. I know pregnant women get a little tetchy, but manners cost nothing.'

'I think I'll just go to bed,' I say.

'I'll tell you what you're going to do. You're going to get dressed and go shopping for an outfit for Shoni's wedding.'

'I don't think I'm invited.'

'Rubbish. She'll be fine, once she's had time to calm down.'

'About three years.'

Chapter 23

Two Months Later

#fatasfuck

So, we're in town. I'm in a changing room trying to fit my pregnant torso into a maternity gown for midgets when I hear a familiar voice.

'Mick, how lovely. Yes, I'm with Roberta. She's trying on a dress for the wedding.' If he makes a joke about a tent or a marquee, I swear I will bite off his extremities one by one. The bump is huge. I can't breathe it in anymore.

'How is she?' I hear him say.

'So so,' Tammy says.

'I'm fine,' I say, sweeping back the curtain and showing my pregnant hump in all its glory. 'I think I need a bigger size.' He stares. Rude. Still staring.

'Jesus, Bob, who'd you swallow?' I might have bloody known.

'She's pregnant,' Tammy says. His face says it all. Shock. Horror. Revulsion.

'Oh, so, that's why you're getting married. I did wonder.' What the heck is he talking about? Me, getting married? As if I'd be so bloody stupid again. I don't have time to correct him before he turns and disappears.

'One way of getting rid of him,' I say.

A text comes through from Mick: 'I hope ul b v happy 2 gether.'

'He must think I'm marrying Harry McGarrigle,' I say. 'Is he for real? What a douche.'

#tohaveandtohold

Despite all my recriminations about the ostentatious nature of Shoni's wedding, I have to say, the day is perfect. Apart from the waiter dropping soup in my lap and the best man getting drunk and falling on the pageboy, it's going without a hitch. There's a hairy moment when the delegation from Dagenham have an altercation with some lads from Sedgefield, but on the whole, it's a magical day. Shoni smiles throughout, and that, in itself, is a bloody miracle. Knobhead's behaving himself in the main. In that he hasn't tried to molest me, the mother of the groom, or any of the bridesmaids. Dagenham's parents are actually quite nice.

We spend happy evening drinking shots (mocktails for me with a sly shot of gin when no one's looking) and swapping embarrassing stories. Embarrassing for Shoni and Dagenham, whose real name is Kevin John-Joseph Richard Bertram Cunningham. He's not so bad, actually. He sneaks me a couple of glasses of champagne when no one's looking and surprises Shoni with a honeymoon to the Dominican Republic as a wedding present.

I don't like to think about what he might be bringing back, so I'm not going to think about it.

#jobsworth

I'm home from the wedding at last, and my feet are killing me. Heels and pregnancy do not mix. A good time was had by all, and Shoni's safely at the airport on her way to the trip of a lifetime.

Drew rings and says there's a weird bloke keeps hanging round the burger van. Sometimes, he buys something, and other times, he just stands and stares. But then, today, he approached him and said, 'I hope you'll look after Roberta.' Very weird. I ask him for a description, but he says, 'nondescript', which is not very helpful. Who would approach my son and tell him to look after me? I wonder whether it could be the man Carolyn saw hanging around Mother's house. But Carolyn said he was quite tall and quite dark. Drew, when pressed, says, 'Average height, average size and mousey hair.'

***

I'm back at work as there is no longer any need to avoid Mick now that he knows I'm pregnant. It's been a busy couple of weeks. Mick is under the misapprehension that it's me who has been married, and I see no reason to acquaint him otherwise. Let him believe I'm pregnant and married.

I'm looking for Mick as I need him to sign a document before I fax it. His new PA looks down her pointy nose at me.

'Can I help you?' she asks.

'I'm looking for Mick.'

'Mr Vasey is unavailable today.'

'I need him to sign this document. It should have been sent by close of play yesterday.'

'I'm afraid he's unavailable.'

'Can you tell me when he will be available?'

'I'm not at liberty to disclose that information.' For fuck's sake.

'When's he back?'

'As I've said, I'm…'

'I heard what you said. I don't know what it was like in the company you came from, but here, we work as a team.' This isn't altogether true. Some of the departments are full of back-stabbing bastards, but I'm not letting on to her majesty.

'I'll inform Mr Vasey and ensure he gets back to you.'

I'm seething at my desk when Tammy comes to get me for lunch.

'What's up?'

'Miss Fucking Frosty Knickers.' She knows immediately who I mean. 'Won't tell me where Mick is or when he's back.'

'You should have asked me.'

'Well, I would have if I thought you knew.'

'It's a secret,' she says.

'Go on, then.'

'I could tell you, but then, I'd have to kill you.'

'You can tell me over lunch.'

'Ok, but you're buying.'

We're munching on scampi and chips and quaffing mocktails when she tells me, and the bottom falls right out of my world.

Chapter 24

#fucketyfuck

I call in sick. I can't get my head round this. It's too much of a coincidence. But coincidences happen in real life. I feel dirty. I feel disgusted. I feel disgusting. I feel violated.

Tammy told me that the reason Mick is absent from work is because he's seeing an agency about tracing a long-lost relative. Mick. Michael. Oh God. I want to die. It can't be true. Mick the Dick is my brother. This baby I'm having. This thing. It'll probably be born with two heads.

I am never going out again.

I must avoid Mick at all costs.

Tammy texts to ask what the hell happened to me and why was I not at work this afternoon. I ignore her.

***

I'm Googling last-minute deals to some far-flung corner of the world when there's a knock at the door. Tammy's annoying shriek invades my home. I know she won't go away until I let her in, and the pounding is making my head ache.

'Jesus, Roberta. You are becoming so high maintenance,' she says as she bowls through the door, flicks the kettle switch on and pours coffee and milk into cups. 'What the hell happened to you yesterday?'

I toy with the idea of lying to her and telling her that I just had a headache, but I need to share this with someone.

And even though shame burns me, I feel like I have to tell her.

She's speechless. Tammy. Nothing to say. Nicks. Nada. Zilch. Zippo.

'So, you can see why I'm feeling the way I'm feeling.'

'And how are you feeling?'

'How do you think?' I say.

'Is this a quiz? Cos my brain hurts.'

'My everything hurts.'

'What are you going to do?'

'I'm going to do the only thing one can do in these circumstances.' She looks at me blankly. 'I'm going to run away.'

***

I'm on an aeroplane to Paris. I decided just to drive to the airport and see what they had available. I tried to book a flight to Shanghai or Doha. I wanted to get as far away as possible from my home town. The very "helpful" airport employee robot told me I could have a flight to Paris and book a flight further afield from Charles de Gaulle, but they had nothing long haul leaving Newcastle this evening with spare seats.

'If madam can just wait until tomorrow.' No, madam can't. Madam needs to get out of town before she changes her mind, and yes, she does require extra leg room, arse room and belly room. The robot wasn't certain they do extra belly or arse room, but she'd see what she could do about the leg room.

I'm seated next to a man who must have swallowed someone else. He's huge. Mahoosive. Girontonormous. His flab spills over onto my seat, and I find myself squished up against the window. I'm thinking about asking one of the stewardesses to move me when I hear him whisper to one of them, 'Excuse me, I don't mean to be rude, but this lady next to me is taking up rather a lot of room with her stomach. Is there anywhere you could move me to?'

'Are you fucking kidding me?' I ask.

'I beg your pardon?' he says.

'So, you should. You're a man mountain with more peaks than Kilimanjaro, and you have the cheek to tell them I'm squashing you. It's lucky you haven't squeezed this child out of me.' Of course, everyone on the plane is now staring at me. The hostesses are flapping like birds in a fox hole, and I just know I'm going to be on the evening news if I don't bite my tongue.

The girls find him a seat at the front by sweet-talking a little old lady who doesn't need the extra leg room as she only has one. Leg, that is. He waddles to the front. I'm surprised that the plane took off with him on it, and I worry for the rest of the journey about the weight we're carrying.

'They should charge fat people extra,' says the girl in the aisle seat. 'Like, really fat people, I mean. Those who need a crane to get them out of bed.'

'Yeah,' I say. 'Not pretend obese people, like myself, whose doctors are knobheads.'

She gives me a queer look, plugs in her earphones and ignores me for the rest of the flight.

I manage to fly the rest of the way without impinging on anyone else's personal space, and by nine pm, I'm having dinner at the top of the Eiffel Tower. Alone and lonely. The gourmet food is like sawdust in my mouth. I've run away, but the person I'm running from is sitting right with me. The whole of Paris is laid out and lit up before me, and I just want to be back in my own little home, with my own dodgy neighbours and my own feckless and faithless, irritating and abrasive family and friends.

It's when the waiter brings the bill that I feel the pain. And not because it's forty euros more than I expected. A sharp, searing, period type pain. I'm bent double and crying. By the time a paramedic arrives to rescue me, there's a small pool of blood on my chair. Everything turns to black.

#polycephaly

I wake surrounded by white. The baby is still moving inside me, so I know I haven't miscarried. A doctor stands over me running an ultrasound probe over my lower tummy.

'It is as I think,' he says in a sexy French accent.

'What is?' I ask.

'Nurse, Monsieur Diablo, if you please.' I'm sure Diablo means devil, so I'm worried I've died and gone to hell. The nurse frowns, and he says something I don't understand.

'What is it?' I ask him. 'What's wrong?'

'I am seeing something,' he says, peering at the screen, his face impassive.

'What?' I'm panicking now. I know there's something wrong. I never felt so ill with the others. I was never this big with the others. I know I was a lot younger, but this pregnancy feels so different.

'I have seen…there are…how to say…two heads.'

'Oh God. I knew it. I'm having a freak.' Mick must be my brother. I retch, and the nurse runs forward with a bedpan and some tissue.

'Is good news, no?'

'No, of course it isn't.' She obviously doesn't speak very good English.

'Oh, I am sorry,' she says. 'Maybe in time.'

'Maybe in time what?' I'll get over having a baby that looks like an Indian god? I've seen the bloody documentaries. Why did this happen to me? How was I supposed to know?

I cursed Mother and Mick and anyone else who comes to mind.

I'm in the most romantic city in the world, and I've never in my life felt so alone and so lonely. I even wish Tammy was here with her stupid fussing and her idiotic ramblings. When I turn on my phone, I have seventeen missed calls and messages from just about everyone. They range from, 'Hi how r u?' to 'wtf r u playing @'. Why people can't use predictive text, I don't know.

There's an urgent email from Tammy saying, 'Call me re: Mick.' I can't face any more bad news or recriminations. I just want to shut myself away and die.

'We're sending you for a further scan,' the doctor says. 'We've checked the babies' heartbeats, and everything seems to be ok. I would like to make sure of this.'

'It has more than one heartbeat?'

'No, no,' he says. 'Each baby has a heartbeat. They are both beating.'

'I don't understand.'

'Your twins. They are both having heartbeats, but I would just like to see them on the scan, and then, we will let you go home.' He smiles. 'Twice the joy, twice the love, twice the blessing from above.'

It's there in black and white. I'm having twins. Not some two-headed monster freak. They are there on the screen, hugging each other. The medics can't tell the gender because my awkward offspring (no change there) are hiding that part of their anatomy. I don't care. They're healthy and normal. Well, as normal as anyone can be in our weird family.

I decide to go back and face the music. Tell Mick what I know about our parentage and let him decide if he wants to move to outer Mongolia or stay in Newcastle. I'm going nowhere again. I'm staying where I belong.

#noplacelikehome

Tammy's left a voicemail that I only get when my feet are on English soil. Actually, it's tarmac, I think. 'Roberta, you really are a dufus. Ring me when you get this. I need to tell you about Mick.' Ok, I'm ready to face it. I ring.

'Where've you bloody been?' is the first thing she says.

'Paris,' I say.

'Are you kidding me?'

'Nope. I ran away, but I had a bit of a funny turn at the top of the Eiffel Tower, and they rushed me to hospital.'

'Really? Is everything ok? Is the baby?'

'Yeah. You first. What do you want to tell me about Mick?'

'He's not your brother.'

I greet this with silence.

'Do you hear me? He's not Michael. He wasn't looking for a long-lost sister. It's his mother he's trying to trace. He was adopted. His mother is called Doreen, and she emigrated to Bondi Beach. He's an only child. So, you aren't related. As bloody usual, you overreacted.'

The relief feels like hot wee after a long coach journey. I have to sit on the ground for a moment, and a security guard comes running to my assistance.

'Roberta, are you there? Can you hear me?' Tammy's tinny voice says.

'I'm here,' I say, heaving myself to my feet. 'I've got to go. I'll call you when I get home.' This is great news. Brilliant news. Mick and I aren't related. My twins aren't freaks. Oh God. Twins! I'm going to be a single parent of twins at almost fifty. I sit back on the concourse and weep.

Chapter 25

#wrongendofthestick

Drew calls to say could I go to the police station. They've arrested the nutter who's been hanging round the van. He says he knows me.

When I get here, they have Mick in custody. The sergeant is asking if I know him.

'Yes, he's my boss,' I say.

'Is there any reason why he should be hanging round the catering truck?' he asks.

'No,' I say.

'Will you just tell them that you know me and that I'm not a stalker,' Mick says.

'Yes, I know him,' I say. 'Can't vouch that he's not a stalker.'

'Roberta, this is serious,' Mick says.

'It's ok, officer, this man is my boss. He's not a stalker or a weirdo. Well, actually, he is a bit of a weirdo.'

'So, why has he been telling me to take care of you?' Drew asks.

'You have?' I say.

'You must know how I feel about you,' Mick says.

'Yes, you hate me.'

'No, I don't, Roberta. I don't hate you at all. Whatever gave you that impression?'

'Er, *you* did. You constantly wind me up and call me names and make jokes.'

'Exactly, I make jokes. It's banter, Bob.'

'Stop calling me that. Jokes are supposed to be funny.'

'I'm sorry.'

'So you should be. Just because you hate me doesn't mean you should always be trying to humiliate me.'

'I'd never try to humiliate you, Roberta, and I don't hate you. Quite the opposite, in fact.'

'What's that supposed to mean?'

'It means I like you. I like you very much.'

'Oh.'

'I've liked you since the day we met. The weekend we spent in Harrogate was great, but then, the next day, you acted like you were horrified, and you wanted to forget what happened…'

'Oh no. You are not pinning that on me. You acted like you were ashamed and embarrassed to be seen with me.'

'Mother, do I need to listen to this?' Drew says.

'Mother?' Mick says. 'He's your son?'

'Yes.'

He shakes his head. 'So, who did you marry?'

'I didn't marry anyone.'

'But the wedding–'

'My daughter's.'

'Why didn't you say?'

'Not my fault you got hold of the wrong end of the stick.'

'I called you and called you, and you ignored my calls. You didn't reply to any of my texts,' he says. 'And then you were meeting that Harry bloke.'

'He was just an ex and he's going to remain an ex. I can't stand him.'

'And then, I came to your place, and you were with your ex-husband. I thought you were just a player, then, so I backed off.'

'My ex-husband was staying in my house because he had nowhere else to go, and there's a deed of trust on the property.

I didn't want to get into any court battle with him, so it was easier to let him stay. I haven't been romantically involved with him for years, and I threatened to remove parts of his body if he came anywhere near me when he stayed there. I threw him out because I caught him shagging Perfect Pam on my sofa.'

'Oh. Then, I saw that you were working in the catering van and assumed the young man was your partner in more ways than one.'

'You shouldn't have assumed – and why were you telling him to look after me?'

'Just because I couldn't have you didn't mean I didn't care what happened to you.'

'You are such a douche bag. You haven't been hanging round my daughter's place at Durham, have you?'

'No,' he says, horrified. 'I'm a friend, not a stalker.'

'And you haven't been sending weird emails?'

'Not guilty. I like you, I'm not obsessed with you.'

'Like as in…'

'Like as in this,' he says. And kisses me. Properly. With tongues. And I like it. I like it a lot.

'Get a room,' Drew and the sergeant say in unison.

***

So, that's what we do. We get a room. At Malmaison.

'So, the baby?' Mick says as we're lying on the bed eating strawberries and drinking champagne. Well, he's drinking champagne, and I'm eyeing it jealously and taking a sly sip when he goes to the bathroom.

'Is yours,' I say.

'Blimey,' he says, and smiles.

'It's twins,' I say.

'Are you winding me up?'

'Nope.' He smiles again.

#loveisintheair

I won't tell you what Mick and I got up to at Malmaison. Suffice to say, I could probably be having sextuplets now. I know you're going to make snide remarks about me hating him and calling him a dick. And, yes, you're right, but love and hate are two opposing sides of the same coin. And I only hated him because I felt rejected after Harrogate. I thought he'd just humped me and dumped me. Turns out, he thought the same thing.

So, now, we're a couple. The kids, of course, are a little bit horrified, but, as Shoni says, at least her brothers or sisters won't be "total little bastards". And it'll give her some practice for when she has her own. Tammy is bemused and keeps suggesting double dates with her and the Foetus.

Indigestion is a very burning issue at present. Literally. I'm quaffing Gaviscon like the cast of TOWIE glug champagne. I remember when I was pregnant with Carolyn, and I suffered with terrible heartburn. I resorted once to eating toothpaste, which didn't help, but it did make the morning sickness more bearable. Mother said it was a sure sign the baby had loads of hair. When she was born bald as a billiard ball, I realised that most old wives' tales were basically bullshit. "It's all at the front, must be a boy." "Eat lots of fish and you'll have a girl." Also, not true, but I smell like a mackerel. "Lie on the floor and dangle a wedding ring over your belly. If it circles to the right, it's a girl. If it circles to the left, it's a boy." What if it just moves up and down? What if it doesn't move?

Mick the di…delicious, desirable, delightful and I are moving in together. I know Patti tells us not to cohabit unless you have a ring on it, but I'm not in the first flushes of youth (BTW I didn't notice any flushes in youth, they all arrived with middle age, so not sure what that saying means). We decide he'll move into my place but keep his own flat so that he can disappear if we get on top of each other, or when we don't want to get on top of each other, or when I have raging hormones and I think I might kill him.

***

My Facebook updates say things like "feeling blessed" and "feeling loved", just like all those twatty people I generally hate. I've drawn the line at photographing our dinner and posting that online, but my gushings are beginning to get on my own nerves. I've become half of one of those self-satisfied smug couples who laugh in the face of sad-sack singles everywhere. Hahaha to those going speed dating, hohoho to those on eHarmony, heeheehee to the Grindr and Tinder crew. I'm now one half of a whole couple.

You'd think I'd be happy. You'd think I'd be relaxed, but oh no. Not me. Now that I've finally fallen in love and found someone I want to share my life with, I've developed an overwhelming feeling of fear, paranoia and insecurity. Now, my days are consumed with the idea that Mick will do what Knobhead did. Not necessarily with Terri-Ann from Thomas Cook (I don't think Mick is her type, on account of him being the opposite of Knobhead). But I'm waking up feeling anxious that he will meet somebody else and run off with her, leaving my heart shattered into a million different pieces.

I find myself listening in to his conversations with women from work for signs that he wants them. If he mentions a woman's name, my gut churns, and I wonder if he fancies her. Before I know it, my imagination has run away with me, and he's having a full-blown affair, is leaving me and getting married to someone else.

Everywhere I look, there are young, pretty, tanned, toned, topless beauties, and I feel fat, frumpy and middle-aged. Why would Mick want to be with me when he could have any young woman he wanted?

I'm working on a proposal for our newest client when Mick's phone dings from the table where he's left it on charge. Immediately, I'm imagining it's someone he wants to date. I picture a tall, leggy blonde with tanned skin and a designer dress. I'm torn between checking who the message is from and respecting his privacy. I respected Knobhead's privacy and look where that got me. An internal dialogue begins. The devil is telling me to look: *It's justified, you don't want to be humiliated again*. The angel chastises me: *A relationship is nothing without trust, you have no right to check his mail.* The devil: *What's the harm, just set your mind at rest.* The angel: *He loves you, he doesn't want anyone else, he's told you so*. Devil: *Knobhead told you that and look what he was up to.*

I pick up the phone, my stomach churning, my hands shaking. The text is on the screen. It's from someone called Simone. I immediately imagine an exotic beauty, with legs up to her ears and perfect white teeth: 'Thanks for yesterday, babe, you're a star. Maybe we should…' The rest of the message doesn't show. Maybe they should do what? What did he do yesterday? Oh no! That's it, he's having an affair. My blood runs cold. Now what am I going to do? If I confront him about it, he'll know I've been snooping.

Devil: *It wasn't snooping, it was self-preservation, you were only trying to set your mind at rest*. Angel: *You shouldn't have looked, I told you so*. Devil: *You could read the whole message, then delete it. He'll never know you've read it, then, and he won't answer, and Mrs Longlegs might take the huff and never contact him again.* Crap. What do I do?

I click on the message to read the rest of it. 'Maybe we should do a foursome one night. Me and Dave and you and Roberta. Let me no.' I hate people who use "no" for "know".

Fuck. I hear the chain flushing and his footsteps in the hall. I delete the message and sit the phone back exactly where it was, sitting down on the sofa and pretending to flick through the channels for something to watch.

'Was that my phone?' Mick asks.

My cheeks burn. 'Think so,' I say.

'Strange,' he says, picking it up and flicking through. 'I thought I heard the message tone.'

'Maybe it was mine,' I say, rifling through my bag. 'Oh, yes, I've a message from Tammy.'

'What's she say?' he asks. My mother always told me if you tell one lie, it escalates into another and another.

'Nothing much. Same old, same old.' My hands are still shaking, and I'm sure he can tell I'm lying. I must never do that again. Never. Ever.

The next time it happens, I have no control over myself and my emotions. Every time his phone dings, my heart lurches, every time he's online, I'm wondering who he's messaging, every time he goes out of the room to accept a phone call, I turn down the TV and listen at the door. I'm turning into an ex of mine who I ended up hating because he followed my every move and made me feel suffocated. He monitored my phone, my emails, my mail, and I hated it.

***

I've phoned in sick at work as I've been up all-night vomiting. I've managed to drag myself and a duvet to the sofa to watch crappy daytime TV. *Loose Women* has really gone to the dogs. If that slapper of a page three girl talks about her nether regions once more, I'm going to write to ITV, and if the least talented Nolan sister pulls that face again, I'm gonna stick my foot through the telly.

I send Mick a message telling him I miss him. When did I get so soft and slushy? A flashing light from the corner of the room catches my eye, and I realise Mick has left his phone. The devil tells me to check it. Read his messages. Make sure he isn't playing away. Maybe he's not at work today. Maybe he's taken a buxom beauty to a hotel room. The angel tells me to stop being ridiculous. A relationship is nothing without trust. Mick loves you. He tells you every day he loves you. He isn't doing anything wrong. He's at work. Ring the office to speak to him. I ring, and his secretary puts me through.

'Hi, hun. I'm a little busy right now, can I call you back?'

'You left your phone at home,' I say.

'I know,' he says. 'Just turn it off, if it's disturbing you. I'm just taking a client to lunch, and I'll call you when I'm back at the office.'

'Which client?' I ask, just knowing it will be some attractive woman.

'Melanie Abbot from Franksome's,' he says. My gut immediately starts to churn. Melanie is five feet nine with plastic tits and straight white teeth. She and Mick used to go out for a while a few months ago. I feel a surge of fear which immediately turns to anger.

'Enjoy lunch with your ex,' I snap before cutting the call and throwing my phone across the room, smashing the screen. Shit. I pick it up and burst into tears. My phone rings, and Mick's office number appears on the cracked screen. I ignore it. He rings four more times, and I continue to ignore him. I feel like a thirteen-year-old girl. An email comes through. 'Answer your phone, please. What's wrong? It's just lunch, Roberta! She's a client.'

I know I'm being ridiculous. I can't justify my actions. I hate how I feel. I want to scream. I spend the next hour agonising that he and Melanie are flirting, drinking, and end up booking into a hotel room. I cry, I throw up, I cry some more. By the time Mick comes home, my eyes are red, and I feel like a dishcloth.

'Jesus, Roberta, what's wrong?'

'Nothing,' I say. 'I'm going to bed. Did you enjoy your lunch?'

'Roberta, what's the problem? It was a business lunch. There's nothing between Melanie and I.'

'Well, you used to fancy her.'

'In the past,' he says.

'She's very attractive.'

'If you like that kind of thing,' he says. 'Are you questioning my integrity?'

'No.'

'Do you think I'm just going to go out and sleep with every attractive woman I meet?'

'You did before.'

'That was before I was in a relationship. When I'm in a relationship, I don't mess about. I'm hurt, Roberta, that you would even think it.' The tears start again. He hugs me. 'I just want you and no one else.' I feel reassured and happy. I'm an idiot. He doesn't fancy Melanie. He doesn't want anyone else, he's happy with me. I fall asleep happy and content in his arms.

If only that feeling of contentment would last. As soon as he leaves for work the next day, all the insecurities come flooding back. I feel fat, frumpy and bloated. My hair's a mess, my nails are brittle, my legs need shaving. Beautiful young things cavort on *Love Island* making me feel old and unattractive.

The house phone rings, and I let the answerphone click in. I'm too ugly to talk to anyone. Melanie Abbot's sexy tones slither through the sitting room. 'Mick, daahling, great to catch up with you yesterday, yah. Let's do it again, sweetie.' My stomach flips, my hands shake. I pick up the phone and scream, 'FUCK OFF,' into the mouthpiece. I feel better for about three seconds, then shame overwhelms me. I cry again. I've turned into someone else. Where has the self-contained, composed, emotionless woman gone? I want her back. I feel like my body and brain have been invaded by a tragic teen emo.

The phone rings again, and Mick's voice, concerned and serious, enters the house. 'Hi, Roberta, if you're there will you pick up please. Melanie rang and apparently someone screamed obscenities at her. Maybe she got a wrong number, but I just wanted to check in on you. Love you.'

I wait five minutes and ring him. 'Sorry, baby, I was in the shower. What's this about Melanie?'

'She rang my mobile. She'd tried me at work, and someone had erroneously told her I was at home today. She rang the house phone and got a load of abuse, apparently.' My face burns. Lying bitch. Load of abuse. It was one big fuck off, that's all.

'Like I said, I was in the shower, and I didn't hear the phone. She must have got a wrong number.' I'm now wondering why Melanie has his mobile number and the house phone. I try to bite my tongue, but my devil won't let me. 'How come she has the home number?'

'No idea,' he says. 'Maybe someone at work gave it to her.'

I want to tell him to tell her to go to hell, but I know I'm being unreasonable. 'I don't like her,' I blurt out. 'I don't want her having my number.'

'Oh,' he says. 'I didn't realise you two didn't get along.'

'Can't stand her,' I say.

'She can be a bitch,' he says. 'But the contract is really important so…'

'More important than me?' I ask. Why can't I bite my tongue? What the hell am I doing?

'What? Roberta, what are you talking about? No contract is as important as you. What's going on with you? Are you hormonal?' For some reason, his question incenses me. I want to scream and rail and cry. 'I'm going,' I say.

'What's up?'

If you don't know, I'm not going to tell you. 'Nothing,' I say.

'I'll see you tonight.'

'Whatever.'

'What do you mean, whatever? Don't you want me to come over?'

'Do you want to come over?'

'Jeez, you're such hard work today.'

My temper soars again. 'Go and see Melanie instead, then. I've heard she's really easy.' I slam down the phone and burst into tears again.

Half an hour later, Mick is letting himself in the front door. I'm eating ice cream and listening to REM.

'For the last time, Roberta. There is nothing going on between Melanie and me. I don't fancy her, I don't want her. What do I have to say or do to make you believe me? I feel like you're doubting me and that hurts.'

'You're a player,' I say.

'Used to be,' he says. 'When I'm in a relationship, I stay faithful.'

'That's what they all say.'

'Meaning?'

'I've heard it all before.'

'So, you're judging me by the sins of your former boyfriends and husband. That's not fair.' He's right, of course, it isn't fair. 'You wouldn't like it if I judged you by the mistakes past girlfriends have made. You'd go ape shit if I did that.'

I would, he's right. How do I stop feeling like this? It's killing me. All I want him to do is to hug me and tell me everything will be alright, but I'm as prickly as a thistle so why would he want to?

'Changing the subject, I've got a leaflet for an antenatal class at the Crown Hotel. It's run by an expert in prenatal care.'

'I hate to break it to you, Mick, but I have done this three times before.' I take the leaflet and see the class is run by a man.

'Yes, Roberta, but I haven't, and I'd really like to go.'

'You go, then,' I say.

'It would be good for you. It incorporates pregnancy yoga.'

'I'd rather eat my own entrails.'

'Come on, Roberta, don't knock it until you've tried it.'

'The last thing I'd like to do is go to a class where a ten-year-old boy mansplains to me how to push my offspring through my own vagina while listening to whale music. When a bloke can push a basketball through the end of his urethra, I might listen to him about giving birth.'

'If you don't like it, we'll leave immediately. I promise.'

'No. Absolutely not. Never in the history of the creation of all creatures great and small. Out of the question. No. Nein, Non. Nil. Nope. Nah. Never.'

***

We're upstairs at the Crown for the antenatal class. The flyer said to wear something you find it easy to move in, but I feel so heavy, I can hardly move in anything. I'm wearing maternity leggings and a long tunic and sitting next to a girl who's wearing a green bikini top and thong. Apparently, it's a thing to let everything hang out. That might be ok when you're seventeen and six stone soaked through, but I'd have looked like Lumpy Ridge in summertime. I'd have been arrested for crimes against corneas. The reception is soon filled with pregnant women of all shapes, sizes and colours.

We're given name badges and ushered into a carpeted room by bottle-blonde baby doll Brenda. Bottle-blonde Brenda "call me Bren" tells us to find a floor cushion and lie in a relaxed position against our baby daddy. Two girls put their hands in the air. They're wearing matching grubby tracksuit bottoms and have three teeth between them. They wouldn't even make the auditions for Jeremy Kyle.

'We don't have a baby daddy,' the dark one says.

'Would you mind sharing?' Call-me-Bren says to me and Mick.

'Yes, I bloody well would,' I say.

'I don't mind,' a mousey girl wearing a tent says. 'Howard will happily stand in.' Poor Howard looks like he'd happily do nothing of the sort, but Christine has volunteered him now, so it's too late.

'I must apologise for the absence of our expert. His wife is about to give birth. You'll have to make do with me, I'm afraid,' Call-me-Bren says. Frankly I'm glad. If someone is going to tell me how to push things through my vagina, they should at least be in possession of one themselves.

We're lying like something from *The Handmaid's Tale*, and Call-me-Bren is telling us to breathe. 'Well, I wasn't thinking of stopping for some time yet, you daft tart,' I mutter under my breath, only Call-me-Bren has hearing like a bat.

'What was that, Bertha?' she says. I realise she's talking to me. Unless she has a wonky eye and is looking at the girl behind.

'The name's Roberta,' I say.

'Oh, your name badge is wonky,' she says.

Just like your eye.

'Let's get down to business,' she says. 'The first thing I want to talk about is the common misconception pregnant women have that they're going to give birth to a baby.'

I roll my eyes.

'Roberta!' Mick says. 'Be patient.'

'You're not just giving birth to a baby...you're actually giving birth to parents.'

'Aw for f–'

'Roberta.'

'I can't stand any more of this crap,' I say to Mick, struggling to extract myself from between his legs and sticking an elbow in his delicate area. He yowls like a cat that's been stood on, and the rest of the ladies stifle giggles.

'Show of hands, please – how many people are in partnered relationships? Anybody else flying solo?' Call-me-Bren continues, ignoring our outburst. *Way to go, Brenda. How to make people feel inadequate.*

'Roberta, you promised to try,' Mick hisses.

'And you promised if the class was crap and I hated it, we would leave,' I say loudly, amid gasps from the other women.

Call-me-Bren ignores us and continues to talk about pregnant women in nomadic cultures and squatting. I manage to switch off and let my mind wander so that Mick can listen to all the bullshit.

Half an hour later, Call-me-Bren gets out the rubber babies and the giant cervix. As one of the babies is being pushed through the cervix, the men start dropping like dominoes. Howard is first to turn green and hit the deck, shortly followed by Mick and a boy at the front who doesn't look old enough to tie his shoelaces. When Mick has drunk a cup of hot sweet tea, he doesn't take much persuading to retire to the bar, instead of listening to the delivery of the afterbirth. We begin a mass exodus which Call-me-Bren tries to ignore. Everyone but Howard and Christine turn up in the bar downstairs. I manage to get the barman to sneak a vodka in my orange while Mick is at the loo. It takes the edge off a little.

Chapter 26

#beingnice

I'm stressing about my relationship with Mick. I don't feel worthy. I don't think I deserve to be happy. I blame my mother, in part. She was so cold, so unavailable – which I do now understand, to a degree. The letters served to inform me why she was the way she was and went some way to helping me to forgive her. To some degree, I'd done the same thing myself.

I haven't always been this hard. When I first had my children, I was loving and warm. I was married and happy. I was a good person. I want to be a good person again. I've forgotten what it's like to be nice. I haven't been nice since Knobhead walked out to be with Terri-Ann from Thomas Cook. I've grown to hate everything. I became disgruntled, dissatisfied and impatient. I convinced myself I hated everyone and everything. I've been cold with my kids and hard on my colleagues. I am out of practice being nice, but I'm going to try. I really want this relationship with Mick the Di…Delicious to work.

'What do you think of my new jacket?' he says today as he breezes in wearing a thing that looks like it should be wrapped around a hobo (oops, sorry, PC brigade. I promised to be nice) – a homeless person (who I'm sure is not a drug addict or alcoholic and who probably lost his home through no fault of his own in some tragic family break-up caused by small business failure in the recession. So therefore, it is not his fault but David Cameron's, Theresa May's, or Gordon Brown's, depending on your political stance).

Normally, in circumstances such as these, I would be unable to tell a lie. I would have to tell him he looks like something the cat shat. The shiny new improved Roberta, however, says, 'Er…lovely…er, jacket.' He looks disappointed. I cannot gush, but I will try. 'Suits you… brings out the…er…rusty quality of your eyes.'

'Ok,' he says in a manner that suggests he's taken offence. I must practise being nice. It doesn't come easily. I've been grumpy for so long, it's become second nature. He hands me a copy of a novel he's been reading. 'I've finished this. Read it and let me know what you think,' he says. I bloody hate Parsons, but I take it.

'Lovely,' I say. He looks at me strangely. I'm no good at this.

'I'll make dinner, shall I? Tuna pasta bake ok?' I loathe tuna pasta bake. Disgusting mess of rancid goo.

'Er…yes, that would be lovely,' I lie. Mick narrows his eyes and disappears into the kitchen. He knows I'm lying. I must gush when he's made the ghastly gunk. I can hear him chopping and cursing. 'Do you need a hand?' I ask.

'I'm fine,' he says. 'Fucking onions.' When I enter the kitchen, he has a small towel wrapped round his bleeding hand.

'Run it under the cold tap,' I say, taking his arm and sticking it under.

'I said I'm fine,' he snaps. The hurt must show on my face even though I pride myself on being impassive. 'What's wrong, Roberta?'

'Nothing,' I say. Still trying to gush. 'Everything is perfectly peachy.' When I sit down to the rancid pasta shit-mix, I beam. 'Mmm, delicious.' Mick slams down his fork and gets to his feet. 'Where are you going?' I ask. He must know I'm lying. I must try harder to be nice.

'I've just remembered, I have to work.' He pulls on his coat and has left before I can attempt to stop him. I can't do this. The being nice is killing me, and I'm obviously not doing it properly. He's going to leave me for some bubbly airhead who'd smile if her arse was on fire. Double fuckety fuck.

#selfhelp

I usually think people who read self-help books and have life coaches are twats. Yet I find myself this afternoon sneaking round the shelves of Waterstones looking for something that might teach me to be nice. *A More Pleasant You* looks like it could have been written for the occasion. I impulse buy it, stuff it inside a bag so no one can see the cover and read the title, then toddle upstairs to the coffee shop to begin to read.

There's a queue, as usual, and the assistants in here are famously slow (yes, I mean in mind as well as in body). A red-haired girl with a pierced lip takes half an hour to lay a napkin on a saucer, and I want to throw myself out of the upstairs window. There's a mother and baby in front of me. The baby has a mixture of snot and chocolate smeared round its fat face. Whoever thinks these things are cute wants shooting. They yowl and spew runny green stuff from their orifices at regular intervals. They keep you up all night so you feel like you've been in a Japanese sleep deprivation experiment. They ruin every adult conversation you ever attempt to conduct. What's to like?

The mother, who has obviously had her brain turned to mush by staying at home with the snotty spew machine, can't decide between an Emmenthal and mushroom toastie with béchamel sauce, mozzarella and mature cheddar, and a Very Berry Skinny Muffin with a Mocha Chocolate (yaya). (I added the *yaya* and sang the tune to Lady Marmalade in my head). FUCK OFF! I want to scream.

Except everyone turns to look at me because I have really screamed, 'Fuck off' and not just thought it. Although my stomach is rumbling and I'm desperate to read my self-help purchase, I mutter something about having Tourette's Syndrome, and I'm considering reporting them all for disability hate crime and swoop out in a dignified exit. I say dignified; I trip over the display of *Fifty Shades of Grey* and fall down the stairs, hitting every step with my ample bottom.

The woman standing next to the one who sold me the book comes running to help, but I know she's only afraid I'll sue them in a "had an accident in the last three years that's not your fault?" kind of way.

'I'm fine,' I say.

'Would madam like a glass of water?'

'Why? Is that going to help the huge bruise I have growing on my arse?'

She looks embarrassed. So, she should, offering me H_2O when I need an ice pack and a burka. For some stupid, insane reason, I feel like I'm going to cry. That is just pathetic. People who cry when they bruise their pride, or their bottom, are just tragic. The book falls out of the paper bag I shoved it in, and I see her glance at the title. She looks knowingly and says, 'Enjoy the book.'

'It's not for me,' I say.

'Really?' she says.

'Really,' I say, making sure she knows I'm looking at her name badge. Only I can't see her name properly as the blurred visions started again. Crap! I've probably got a brain tumour. I quickly get to my feet and pat myself down. She sees the bump.

'Oh,' she says. 'I didn't realise.'

'Realise what?' I say.

'That you are pregnant.'

'I'm not,' I say. She looks like she wants to crawl under the bookshelf and stay there until she dies. This is fun.

'Oh…I'm so sorry… I thought…'

'Thought what? Just because I've gained a couple of pounds, you think I'm pregnant? Are you always this rude?' Hahaha.

'I'm really sorry… I…' She's struggling. I stare at her expectantly. 'I'm dreadfully sorry.'

'So, you should be.' My work is done here. I swoop out tucking my "be nice" book under my arm.

#tryingmybestffs

Of course, when I tell Tammy about my bookshop escapade, she says I'm an evil bitch. 'Thank you,' I say.

'Being nice didn't last long, Roberta,' she chides.

'It's no fun,' I say.

'Must try harder,' she says.

I wait until I'm in bed that night to open the book. The blurb says it's a practical guide to "Start your own nice revolution". I've always liked the idea of a revolution. That's why I thought this book might be for me. I could have picked up *Nice Girls Can Come First,* but I wasn't sure whether that was a sex guide or a life guide. I almost picked *How Nice Is Your Aura*, but I thought it would have been one of those twatty, astrological wank-fests that Tammy would enjoy. Uranus rising in your full moon type crap. Beware a man in uniform in a white car. Yes, cos he'll probably give you a parking ticket.

There was one called *Being Genuine*. But being genuine is what my problem is. I tell people what I genuinely think, and they just think I'm a bitch.

'Be the best version of you,' says the book. 'Forget about wishing for better and concentrate on making it better.

Tips in order to do this. 1. Get educated. 2. Improve your person.' (Perhaps it means get Botox and have your teeth whitened) '3. Get back your credibility. 4. Spend more time with your family. 5. Be the first person in work and the last person to leave.'

You see, that's what I hate about these self-help books. They're contradictory. How can you spend more time with your family if you're the first person into work and the last person to leave? And would I really want to spend more time with Shoni, Carolyn and Drew? Would they really want to spend more time with me? I doubt it.

Ooh, this bit looks interesting. There's an online forum for people who are having problems being nice. I logon to my computer and type in the URL. A cheap-looking site pops up with an advert for earwax solutions running down the side (Note: the earwax isn't running, the advert is). The site is called PsychsRUs.com. There's a picture of an angel across the top of the page with its arms reaching round the whole site. Just the kind of crap I loathe.

The first thread could actually have been written by me. "Why do I hate everyone?" it asks. It's written by someone called Odbob and moderated by Queeram and Poodle.

'So, a few months ago now,' it begins, 'I realised that I hate almost everyone in my life. The people I work with, my "friends", my family, the people on public transport, the people who serve me in shops. Stupid people irritate me, I don't find funny people humorous, and I could punch my family members repeatedly. I anger very easily, and I cannot take criticism of any kind. Everyone else is always wrong and I am always right. Am I a pathological narcissist?'

Steady on, I wouldn't go that far. You're just a bit grumpy sometimes by the sound of it, I thought. You don't have a psychiatric disorder. That's the trouble with today's society; everyone wants a label. Some people just write in to these forums for attention. Nevertheless, I'm intrigued by the responses. You have to scroll down to get the answers, and there's a button which, when I click on it, takes me to a link that asks me for my details. I know I'm going to be inundated by phone calls about PPI, but I can't resist finding out what people think of this person.

One unhelpful reply says: 'Yeah, mate, your a sicko and a weirdo. Go kill yourself.'

Underneath, someone has typed: 'And *you* can't spell you're so *you're* the thicko.'

The next reply is written by someone calling themselves Archbish 22. It says: 'You have many of the personality traits of someone with Narcissistic Personality Disorder, but I would say I need to know more about you to be able to diagnose this conclusively.'

Diagnose it conclusively? After an online chat? Moron. I want to type, you have the handle of someone with no personality and no sense of humour, but instead, I read on.

'Was your mother cold and unfeeling? Did you feel emotionally detached? Was she emotionally abusive? Did you grow up feeling unloved?'

Odbob replies: 'Yes, my mother was a dragon. Nothing I ever did was good enough. There was no love, no cuddles, no affection.'

Archbish says: 'I think narcissism and misanthropy are a defence mechanism against the ill-content you have about your upbringing. I suggest you see a therapist.'

What utter garbage, I think, slamming the laptop screen down and flinging the book across the bed. Bloody American drivel. What a waste of £13.99.

I check my emails on my phone. There's one from the site I've just been reading. They've sent me the thread. Someone is asking: 'Have you been cheated on by a loved one, as this can cause these feelings of hatred towards everyone?' Argh! I delete the email and throw the phone across the room, instantly regretting it. I run to pick it up and check the screen. There are no more cracks than the last time I threw it, thankfully. A red number on my mailbox alerts me to the presence of a message. It's Mick.

'What do you think of the new Parsons book?'

Now, I think this book is badly written, over sentimentalised, puerile bullshit and I'm struggling to get beyond the first couple of chapters, but I'm being nice, so I type, 'Yeah it's ok.'

'Oh,' he types. 'G2G'

At one time, I'd have sent a sarcastic message about the ridiculous use of acronyms and abbreviations. But I'm being nice.

#normalserviceisresumed

Mick is being weird. He says he wants to talk to me. I know he's going to break up with me because I can't be nice.

'Why don't we have a seat?' he asks.

'I'd rather stand,' I say.

'Roberta, sit down please.' I sit. I never do as I'm told, but I remember I'm supposed to be being nice and maybe obedience comes under being nice. He runs his hand through his hair and bites his lip. 'It's just not working out.'

'What isn't? World peace?'

'Come on, Roberta, you know what I mean. Me and you. Us. It just isn't working.'

I want to scratch out his eyes. 'I don't know what you mean. I think we're getting on really well.'

'You're not the person I thought you were.'

'I can change,' I say. I never thought I'd hear myself say that, but I want to be with him, and if that means trying to be nice, then that's what I'll be.

'You're just not what I thought–'

'I can try... I–'

'You're just too...'

'Look, I know I'm...'

'You're just too nice.'

'Nice?' I shriek, incredulous. 'Nice? Me? Are you fucking kidding me? I've been trying my best to be fucking nice, but your coat makes you look like you crawled out of a maggot-infested skip, your taste in TV programmes makes me want to remove my own eyeballs and ears with a pitchfork, and your tuna pasta bake tastes like three-week-old dog shit.'

'Roberta, you're back,' he says.

'What are you talking about, you knobhead?'

He hugs me. 'Thank God, my lovely, acerbic, witty, strong Roberta is back. I thought I was mistaken, and I'd become involved with some weak, pitiful, gushing Stepford Wife. Hurrah.' He spins me round.

'You're making me dizzy, halfwit. Stop it now.'

He kisses me on the lips. 'Don't ever be nice again. You were really freaking me out. Just carry on being you.'

So, that's it. Mick likes me exactly as I am. He doesn't want me to change. I no longer have to bite my tongue and gush. Just as well; gushing definitely is not for me. I have burned the self-help books along with his hobo coat and thrown out seven tins of dolphin friendly tuna.

Chapter 27

#shootmenow

I have a gynae appointment today. Again, I'm sitting next to girls who are younger than my daughters, and their conversation tells me they're worried about stretch marks and cellulite. I, on the other hand, am worried about the end of my existence as a person in my own right. I have become the egg's mother. One girl is talking about how the "sperm donor" unfortunately was pissed and watching the Newcastle game when the momentous discovery was made, so she threw the test at him, and he used it to stir his much-needed coffee. I'd have thrown the telly.

The trouble is, I know what's ahead. These poor fools don't. No one tells you about the all-consuming neurosis that begins sometimes at conception, sometimes at birth. It's all congratulations, fluffy pink towelling things, matching Cosytoes and baby baskets. No one tells you about the worry. The overwhelming anxiety that is parenthood. Why don't they bloody tell you this? It could all have been avoided with the swift application of a rubber. A jonny, my son calls them. A blob, according to the vulgar things I work with. Whoever thought parenthood would be a good idea should be shot with shit.

The horror begins when the little blue minus sign becomes a little pink plus sign. The end of life as you know it. The end of white upholstery. The end of Prada two-pieces (not that I ever began them). The end of intelligent conversation (also as above, although Mick thinks Gaddafi slipping into Jordan is a euphemism for Katie Price's sex life).

#cheaters

I phoned in sick and watched *Cheaters* on daytime TV. It has made me completely paranoid. Mick is acting very strange. I think he's seeing someone else. He's acting just like Knobhead did when he was shagging Terri-Ann from Thomas Cook. I Google: what to do you're your boyfriend is being unfaithful. The site tells me to investigate. Notice suspicious mannerisms. Has he been dressing to impress and wearing more or changing aftershave or cologne? Is he "working late" more often and not telling you what the work is about? Does he check his phone a lot? Has he been withdrawn and distant? Has he been less intimate with you? If the answer to all of these is yes, then he's probably playing away from home.

That's it. He is definitely having an affair. The dick! The devil tells me to check his phone when he gets home. The angel wants me to think carefully about what I'm about to do.

He's late back from work and jumps straight in the shower. Classic signs. His phone is on charge in the kitchen. I pick it up, ignoring the angel. There's a message from someone called Sian. I've never heard him mention her. I feel sick. I put the phone down and check the Sians on his Facebook page. There are three. All bloody attractive. I hate them. I hate him. I pick up his phone and open the message.

"You were bloody amazing" is all it says. The bastard. So, he is screwing around. I knew it. How can I deal with this in a calm, mature way without flying off the handle and ranting like a maniac?

I hear the door and smell his aftershave before he enters the sitting room. The Yankee Candle on my coffee table is flying past his ears before he's managed to park his briefcase on the floor. 'You bastard,' I scream. 'How could you?' Shock makes his mouth a cavern and his eyebrows disappear.

'Roberta, what the f–'

'How could you do that to me? After everything I told you about Knobhead?'

'I have no idea–'

'Don't lie to me.'

'I'm not… I–'

'You were amazing, were you? Get out,' I shriek. 'Get out of my home. You filthy, low-life–'

'Jesus, Roberta, I knew you were a bit nutty, but I didn't think you were totally deranged.' He leaves when I open the cutlery drawer.

I'm back at the website now and it's telling me: Whatever you do, do not overreact. Approach him calmly, let him be heard and be as understanding as possible. Oh crap!

How could I let myself be taken in again, and by him? How could I be so utterly stupid and immature? I've been like an emotional teenager instead of a middle-aged woman. The fury and frustration bubble inside me.

I toss and turn all night, get up and make hot milk, but I still can't sleep. I get up and make whisky. Then, I remember I can't drink whisky because of the babies. The babies are Mick's fault. The bastard. I hate him. Oh God, I love him. I hate him. Text from Mick saying, 'I'm sorry, Roberta.' So, an admission of guilt. The bastard. What is wrong with me? Why can't I keep a man faithful? I must be bad in bed. I must be a terrible human. I am a terrible human. I listen to REM and eat ice cream. I eat cake. Biscuits. Crisps. I order pizza and kebab and chips. I scream into my pillow.

I spend the whole of Saturday and Sunday crying. No more Mrs Nice Guy.

#NHSindirect

Disaster of all disasters. Because I am an almost geriatric pregnant woman (and peri-menopausal) I am apparently in a high-risk group and more likely to have a baby or babies with Down's syndrome or spina bifida. It's bad enough to be procreating at my age without having a child who will need specialist care probably for the rest of its life. I can't do this.

The nurse gives me a leaflet. Reading it makes me feel worse. I am ostensibly more likely to miscarry, have an ectopic pregnancy or a premature birth. I ring NHS Direct. A girl on the other end who sounds like she should be studying for SATS asks me if my lips are blue and whether I am limp or floppy. For fuck's sake.

'Is the patient unconscious?' she asks in a nasal drawl.

'No, I've told you, I am the fucking patient. How can I be unconscious when I'm speaking to you?'

'If madam would like to desist with the profanities, we'll do much better.'

'We'll do much better if you stop asking stupid fucking questions and just answer mine.'

'I won't tell you again, madam. If you persist in abusing me, I shall be left with no alternative but to terminate the call.'

'I would like to ask some questions about pregnancy in older women.'

'The patient is pregnant?'

'Yes.'

'Hold the line please.' Vivaldi's *Four Seasons* squeaks in my ear. I hate that tune. There's a crackle.

'Good afternoon, this is NHS Direct, can I take the patient's name, please.'

'Oh, for fuck's sake.'

'Sorry, madam, it's a bad line. Did you say Mrs Drake?'

'I just want to ask some questions about older women and pregnancy.'

'So, the patient is pregnant?'

'Yes, I am.'

'Does the patient have chest pains?'

'No.'

'Are the patient's lips blue? Are they limp and floppy?'

I slam the phone in its cradle. She'd be limp and floppy with blue lips if I could get hold of her.

I logon to the laptop. You'd have thought a quick phone call would have been easier, but no. Google has taken me to an NHS site. There's a video of a matronly, patronising nurse with white bouffant hair and a mole on her chin telling me not to worry and then listing everything that can go wrong. Sadistic bitch. Now, she's telling me there are societies and support groups to help me if I decide to go ahead with a pregnancy that may result in birth defects. Marvellous. Are they going to move in and change the shitty nappies for the next forty years? I think not. They will however sit around in a circle and moan about how no one understands what it's like to have a special child. How is that any help? If they come and do the washing, that's help. Mow the lawn, help. Spouting crap about the state of the pavements for wheelchairs and the lack of accessible parking facilities or decent special school places, no help at all.

I really wish I hadn't Googled the risks. There's a list as long as a dodgy placenta of things that can go wrong when you're past thirty-five and even more when you're older than forty. Then, at the bottom in blue writing (not sure of the symbolism of this, perhaps it's to represent drowning), it tells me not to be anxious. Anxious? I'm frick fracking apoplectic!

I'm at risk of developing diabetes. Cut out the sugary snacks and drinks. If I don't get my quota of Curly Wurlies, I'll be a maniac. Seemingly, eating a healthy diet, stopping smoking, exercising and cutting out alcohol are all ways I can help mitigate against these risks. They're also ways to make life miserable and unbearable. I put down the packet of chunky KitKats and grab a stick of celery from the fridge. The celery tastes like dog wee, but I persist. It's like chewing a decade old cheese-string. I spit it into a tissue, fling it in the waste-paper basket and rip open a Double Decker.

I bite the bullet and make an appointment with my doctor. He suggests therapy. He says I have issues that I should resolve before the birth of the twins. *You've got issues*, I want to say. *Personal hygiene being one of them.* 'You need to get to the bottom of why you feel the way you do before we can begin to help you.'

'I know why I feel the way I do. People are irksome.'

'Obviously, your hormones are all over the place, so…I'm going to refer you for counselling. It's up to you whether you take the appointment. Good day, Roberta,' he says, standing up. To my horror, I burst into tears. I could slap myself.

He presses a button on his intercom. 'Mary, would you mind bringing me a cup of sweet tea?'

'Of course, Doctor,' says the fawning receptionist, who appears moments later clattering a tray and shoving the door open with her backside. She places it down on the desk (the tray, not her backside), throws a patronising look in my direction and toddles out.

Doctor Lambert pours the tea into a cup, adds milk, and says, 'Sugar?'

I shake my head. 'Sweet enough.'

He rolls his eyes, stirs the brown liquid and hands the cup to me. 'What exactly is the matter, Roberta?'

'You have to ask what the matter is?' I say, taking a sip from the lukewarm tea. 'I'm almost fifty, I'm alone, my kids hate me, my parents are dead, and I'm pregnant with twins to a man who obviously has someone else and despises me.'

'I'm sure your children don't hate you. We often have disagreements with family members, but the bonds between parents and their offspring are the strongest bonds known to man.'

'Which makes me a freak, because I find them hard to like and they find me impossible to love.'

'I'm sure that's not the case. Counselling would help you work through all of these feelings.'

'Would it help my children like me? Would it help me if I give birth to a child with Down's syndrome or spina bifida?'

'Is that what this is about? It's perfectly normal to have reservations about a pregnancy at your age – or any age for that matter. Your fears are very real, but I'm sure you could cope with anything that comes along. God only sends us what we can cope with. You're strong, Roberta. You've proved that time and again. Everything you've been through, and you've never cracked. Many people would break under the strain.' *Oh, God, where are these tears coming from?* 'You can do this.'

Chapter 28

#waterwaterseverywhere

I'm in town on a Friday night with Julian. I told him I wouldn't go to Flares or Sinners under any circumstances in my condition. 'I'm approaching my due date, and I might catch anything from those toilets.'

'Really, Roberta. You cannot catch syphilis from toilet seats.'

'I'm taking no bloody chances.'

How we end up in Gaynor's nightclub, I have no idea. But I feel a searing pain in my back while I'm standing at the bar and retire to the toilet, handing my credit card to Julian and telling him to make sure he doesn't buy the whole bar a round.

I'm in a cubicle leaning against the wall when my waters break. It's a trickle at first, and I think I'm wetting myself due to the pressure of the babies' heads on my bladder. Then, there's a gush and a warm wetness. A puddle appears at my feet. I fall to my knees and try to breathe through the pain. I must be making a noise as there's a knock on the door. 'You ok in there?' says a voice. I groan. 'Do you need some help?'

Another voice says, 'Is she drunk?'

'Not sure.'

'I'm – aaaaaaaaaarrghhhh…'

'She's in pain, whoever she is.'

'Can you open the door for us, love?' says a camp male voice.

I can't reach the handle. The pain has me pinned. I can't speak.

'Hello, love. I'm going to call the fire brigade to get you out. Are you locked in?'

I try to shout. Pain grips me again. Something must be wrong. My labours with the others had built up slowly, beginning with back ache and progressing to unadulterated agony over many hours. This was nought to sixty in ten seconds.

'A…ahhhhhh…ambulance,' I manage.

'What did she say?' says the camp voice.

'Ambulance.'

The loud music and chatter suggest the main door opening, and Julian's voice shouts, 'Roberta.'

'In here. Ahhhhhh.'

'What's wrong? Is it the babies? Where's that water coming from? Oh, God.'

'Get me out of here,' I scream.

'You'll have to open the door.' Oh, God, it can't be. I'm getting the urge to push. Surely, they can't be coming yet. 'You've only been gone half an hour. Surely they can't be on their way?'

I hear ringing and a voice on speakerphone. 'Emergency services, how may I help you?'

'Ambulance, please.'

'Do you think we need the fire brigade to get her out too?' says one of the other voices.

I use every ounce of strength I have to force myself off my knees and from a crouch position. I stretch up to reach the catch and unlock the toilet door. I collapse in a heap, and the door pushes into me.

'Can you move back, Roberta, so that I can get in?'

'No, I can't. Aaaaaaaargh.'

'Just try and move to the side, so I can get in next to you.'

'It's coming,' I say. 'I want to push. Oh, God, I am not having my child in this shithole.'

'Go and get someone to take this door off its hinges,' Julian screams. 'Shall I ring Mick?'

'No, why would you?'

'Because he's the father, and he should be here.'

'No, he shouldn't. He's a liar and a cheat, and I hate him.'

'Roberta, you don't hate him.'

'I do. I hate him, I hate him, I hate him. If you contact him, I will never, ever speak to you again as long as I live. We don't need him. Aaaaargh.' Another pain rips through me. Again, the urge to push. There's a clatter and a bang.

'Which door?' I hear someone say.

'That one.'

'There's a leak,' says the new male voice.

'It's her waters.'

'Just get me out of here,' I scream.

There's a grinding and a scraping, and the door dances before my eyes; a man wearing a penguin suit brandishes a screwdriver. I'm now lying in a heap, in agony.

'Get me out of here,' I repeat. Next thing, I'm being pulled across the floor by my legs and the urge to push is too strong to resist. 'They're coming.'

I'm lying on a cold, tiled floor, surrounded by a dwarf in a hobbit costume, a man in drag with blonde bouffant and red sparkly heels, and a man in a leather waistcoat wearing a butcher's boy cap and lederhosen.

'I never thought I'd be saying this to you, Julian, but get my knickers off.' This has to be the most undignified thing ever to happen to me, and there are many from which to choose.

'Give me your phone,' Julian says.

'We are not going live on Facebook with this,' I shout. 'Someone get on YouTube and find out what we have to do.'

After much pressing of buttons, a soothing voice and music tells us to relax and watch the miracle of birth.

More pain. Burning, searing, stabbing.

'Have a look,' I say to Julian. 'I think they're coming.'

'Oh, God, I can see the head. What shall I do?'

The hobbit takes control. 'Roberta, you're going to have to push.'

'You don't say.' My face is going to burst. The skin around my eyes feels like it's swelling. I imagine I look like a basket of bruised forest fruits. I'm stretching and burning. I feel like I'm going to split in two, like a wooden stake separated by an unforgiving axe.

'Come on, one more push, and baby will be here,' Bilbo Baggins says.

'Aaaaaargh.' I squeeze and push. One more scorching pain.

'The head's out.' I pant, remembering this is what the midwives always told me to do when the head was out. One look at Julian's face sends me into a panic.

'What's wrong?'

'Nothing.'

'Something's wrong.'

'You have a person hanging out of you.' He falls like a felled tree. There's a crack as he hits the tiled floor.

'Where's this fucking ambulance?' the hobbit shrieks. 'Get this knobhead out of here.' A bouncer pulls Julian by his feet, just as he pulled me. The dwarf looks at the screen of her phone.

'Roberta, give me one more push.' The rest of the baby slides out of me in a hot, bloody, wet mess. The dwarf puts down her phone, takes off her jacket and wraps the baby in it.

'Oh God, I can't do that again,' I say.

She looks at me, incomprehension in her eyes.

'It's twins. There's another one in there.'

Her eyes flicker with panic, but she quickly takes control again. Handing the baby to me, she feels down below. 'I can't see the head.' She taps on the screen of her phone.

'You've got to get it out,' I say. 'It'll die. You can't let it die.'

'Shhh, let me read this. I need to find out what to do.' I catch sight of Wikipedia. Oh, God, *I'm* going to die.

'Right, I've got this,' she says.

My head pounds. 'I'm going to be sick.' The man takes off his hat and hands it to me. I retch into the baker's boy cap. My head feels like it's going to explode. Paramedics rush through the doors, just as I'm losing consciousness. Everything turns black.

Chapter 29

#twicethelove

I take a selfie of me and two small humans.

I was unconscious for the birth of my son. My daughter came out no trouble, but you know what the male of the species is like. They're bloody awkward. They have to make a drama out of a crisis. My blood pressure went through the roof, so they used suction and forceps to get him out. They were all a bit scared, apparently. He was a little blue and struggling to breathe, but he soon pinked up and started screaming his lungs out.

I can't believe these perfect little things came out of me. They lie next to my bed in transparent cots, marshmallow soft and squawking like kittens. They're incubated like newborn chicks, a heater above keeping them warm. My son is a little jaundiced. They say it's nothing to worry about, and they're a good size for twins. Especially considering they were a week early. A boy and a girl. Twenty fingers and twenty toes. My undercarriage feels like it's been hit by a truck, and my stomach looks like it's been through a mincer, but I'm inexplicably happy. Carolyn, Shoni and Drew have all been and held them, looking in wonder. Shoni cried. Not the temper tantrum water fest she's wont to indulge in when she's seeking attention but real, emotional tears. Drew kept shaking his head and smiling.

I lift Alice to my breast, and I'm struggling to get her to latch on when I hear a commotion outside.

Mick's raised voice bounces round the ward. 'Don't tell me I can't see my own children.'

'Ms Gallbreath has left explicit instructions that you are not to be allowed to visit. She has every right…'

'What about my rights?' he shouts. 'Roberta! You're not going to get away with this. Let me in for God's sake.' I hear a woman scream, and Mick's voice saying, 'Sorry. I thought my wife was in here.' *Wife, indeed? Who the hell does he think he is?* 'Roberta, where are you?'

'In here,' I say. 'Stop causing a drama.' He pulls back the curtain, and the first thing I notice is that he's unshaven and disheveled. 'Jesus, Mick you look like shit.'

His eyes widen and fill with wonder. 'Are these my twins?'

'No, I borrowed them from the woman in the next bed. She wants them back when they're eighteen. Of course, they're your bloody twins.'

'Oh, Roberta, they're beautiful. Just like you.' He's looking at me with a soppy expression.

'Give over,' I say. 'Stop with the mushy stuff.'

'I love you, Roberta Gallbreath,' he says. 'I know you find that difficult to hear and even more difficult to accept, but I love you, and if I have to climb onto the hospital roof and shout it to the whole city to get you to believe me, I will. I have loved you from that first moment in Harrogate when you were berating the barman for serving me ahead of you when you'd "been waiting all fucking day" and were you "fucking invisible?" I loved you when I transferred over and started managing your team, I loved you when it looked like you were dating anything that moved…'

'I bloomin' wasn't, you cheeky…'

'I know that now, but at the time, you seemed like a right player. I loved you when you were dating everything on Tinder.'

'That was…'

'A mistake?'

'An experiment,' I say.

'Me and you have more chemistry than the rest of them put together.'

'Hmmm, we're like potassium and water.'

'We click,' he says.

'We bang,' I say.

'That's what I love about you.'

'Do you know what I love about you?' I say.

'What?'

'Nothing much,' I say, but I give him a wink, so he knows I'm just joking. 'Only kidding.'

'You can't keep doing that.'

'What?'

'Saying offensive things and then saying "only kidding" so people will forgive you.'

'I've got away with it so far,' I say. 'What about Sian and how amazing you were?'

'She was talking about my presentation to Campbell and Cook's. I secured the contract, and they were originally going to go with Palmer's. When are you going to realise how much I love you, Roberta Gallbreath? I don't want anyone else.' He hugs me, and he kisses the twins. Even with down-below burns, stinging nipples, and my stomach feeling ripped to shreds, I'm happier than I've ever been. I believe him. I think I might be able to trust him.

Epilogue

#familylife

I take a selfie of me, Mick and the twins and upload it to Facebook, Twitter and Instagram. We get 224 likes in a matter of minutes. We are a family. Mick and I are back together. I have become one of the very annoying "feeling contented" people on social media. I may have to slap myself at some point.

Shoni has been every day to see the twins. She stares into the baskets in wonder, and every time they cry, she claims they're the best contraceptive she could ever have.

'Good, I'm far too young to be a grandparent yet,' I say.

Drew brings them inappropriate presents like Spirographs and Scooby-Doo Mystery Machines. The burger van business is going well, and he says he might extend his empire and buy another. 'McDonalds started somewhere,' he says.

Carolyn lifts the twins, even when they're fast asleep, and cradles them, kissing their tiny foreheads. 'We might adopt,' she says.

'We?' I ask.

'Me and Lisa,' she says.

'Oh good,' I say. I think that was my daughter coming out.

'When I've finished my PhD, though.'

'Yes, of course. Unruly toddlers and university don't mix.'

The door opens, and Mick walks in with a bouquet of flowers the size of a tree. I resist the urge to tell him they're a waste of money and will only die. I'm secretly thrilled. I can't see his face for the huge pink and blue bears he's balancing. 'Gender stereotyping already?'

'Not at all,' he says, 'The pink one is for our son, and the blue one is for our daughter.'

Said daughter wakes and screams as though letting us know she approves. Mick smirks. He's the only person in the world who gets me. I can totally be myself. He doesn't judge when I'm grumpy (most days), or when I'm sad, mad or bad (every day).

Personally, I can't stand these "happy ever after" tales. I'm sure there's lots of heartache in store. Mick is sure to turn out to be a serial sheep shagger, and the twins will be ram raiding off-licenses before their sixth birthday. But, just for now, everything is perfect.

It's possible I'll be back to tell you what it's like to be the menopausal mother of terrible twins. The sleepless nights, the hair-greying worry, the impending good school postcode lottery. Maybe you'll want to hear how difficult it is at fifty to function on two hours sleep a night and still work in the city. Doubtless you'll be interested in my dodgy pelvic floor and my lactating breasts. Perhaps you'll be fascinated by my Twitter updates about windy smiles, first teeth and temper tantrums. We also haven't found out who the strange man is who's been hanging around outside Mother's house in Durham or who's sending the strange emails. Maybe they're connected. I intend to do some research when I'm less tied up with two tiny humans.

What I wouldn't give for fourteen hours of uninterrupted sleep, a gin and tonic and a bath alone. Mick must have read my thoughts. He's run a bubble bath for me and hands me a magazine.

'Go and have a soak, I'll see to the monkeys.'

I'm lying in the bubbles, reflecting on my life. One minute, I'm working in the city, dating disastrous men and waiting for the change of life, the next, my life has changed beyond recognition. Who'd have thought I'd be approaching fifty, sitting amid cuddly toys, knee-deep in nappies and enjoying it? I step out of the bubbles and pat myself dry. No time to apply body lotion – strange noises are emanating from the sitting room.

It transpires Michael Junior shat on the sofa, and Alice is screaming for a feed. Mick's face has panic strewn across it. He looks like he's wading through petrol, and someone has struck a match. Bum wipes in one hand and our screaming daughter in the other, he flaps like a menopausal mother hen. I find it cute and endearing. A couple of months down the line and I imagine it will make me want to remove his favourite body parts with a potato peeler.

What advice can I offer you? What pearls of wisdom should I leave you with? An inspirational quote? A time-honored tenet? A meaningful message or word of warning?

#Don't shag a stranger in a hotel room in Harrogate unless you want sick in your Jimmy Choos.

There's a knock at the door. Mick opens it to a man who looks vaguely familiar. 'I'm looking for Roberta Gallbreath,' he says.

'That's me,' I say.

'I don't know whether you've been getting my emails. I think I'm your brother.'